Best Wishes, Happy Holidays
1989
Paul

GREAT MOMENTS IN
FOOTBALL

GREAT MOMENTS IN

FOOTBALL

GEORGE FLYNN

GALLERY BOOKS
An imprint of W.H. Smith Publishers Inc.
112 Madison Avenue
New York, New York 10016

A Bison Book

Published by Gallery Books
A Division of W H Smith Publishers Inc.
112 Madison Avenue
New York, New York 10016

Produced by Bison Books Corp.
15 Sherwood Place
Greenwich, CT 06830

ISBN 0-8317-4026-4

Printed in Hong Kong

1 2 3 4 5 6 7 8 9 10

Page 1: Irresistible force v immovable object. Fordham and Pitt's third scoreless tie, 1937. Page 3: Super Bowl VII, 1973, capstone of Miami's amazing 17-0-0 season.

CONTENTS

6 Introduction
12 Notre Dame Upsets Army: 1913
14 Jim Thorpe and the Beginnings of Pro Football
18 The Four Horsemen
20 The Galloping Ghost
23 Grange Signs with the Chicago Bears
26 The Giants Beat the Bears in Sneakers
31 Notre Dame Beats Ohio State: 1935
34 Baugh Leads the Redskins to the NFL Title
40 The Seven Blocks of Granite and the Dream Backfield
44 The Bears Crush the Redskins: 1940
48 Notre Dame v Army in the Game of the Century
52 Columbia Upsets Army
56 The Browns Beat the Rams: 1950
62 Purdue Upsets Notre Dame

67 Army v Navy: 1950
72 The Colts Beat the Giants in Overtime
80 The Packers Beat the Giants: 1961
87 The Thanksgiving Day Massacre
90 Southern Cal v Wisconsin: The Greatest Rose Bowl?
94 The Packers v the Cowboys
97 The First Super Bowl
102 The Green Bay Packers' Third NFL Title
108 The Jets Come to Super Bowl III
113 The Miraculous Reception
116 Miami's Unbeaten Season: 1972-3
121 The Best Super Bowl
126 The Chargers v the Dolphins in the 1982 AFC Semi-finals
135 Michigan v Ohio State: 1986
143 Index

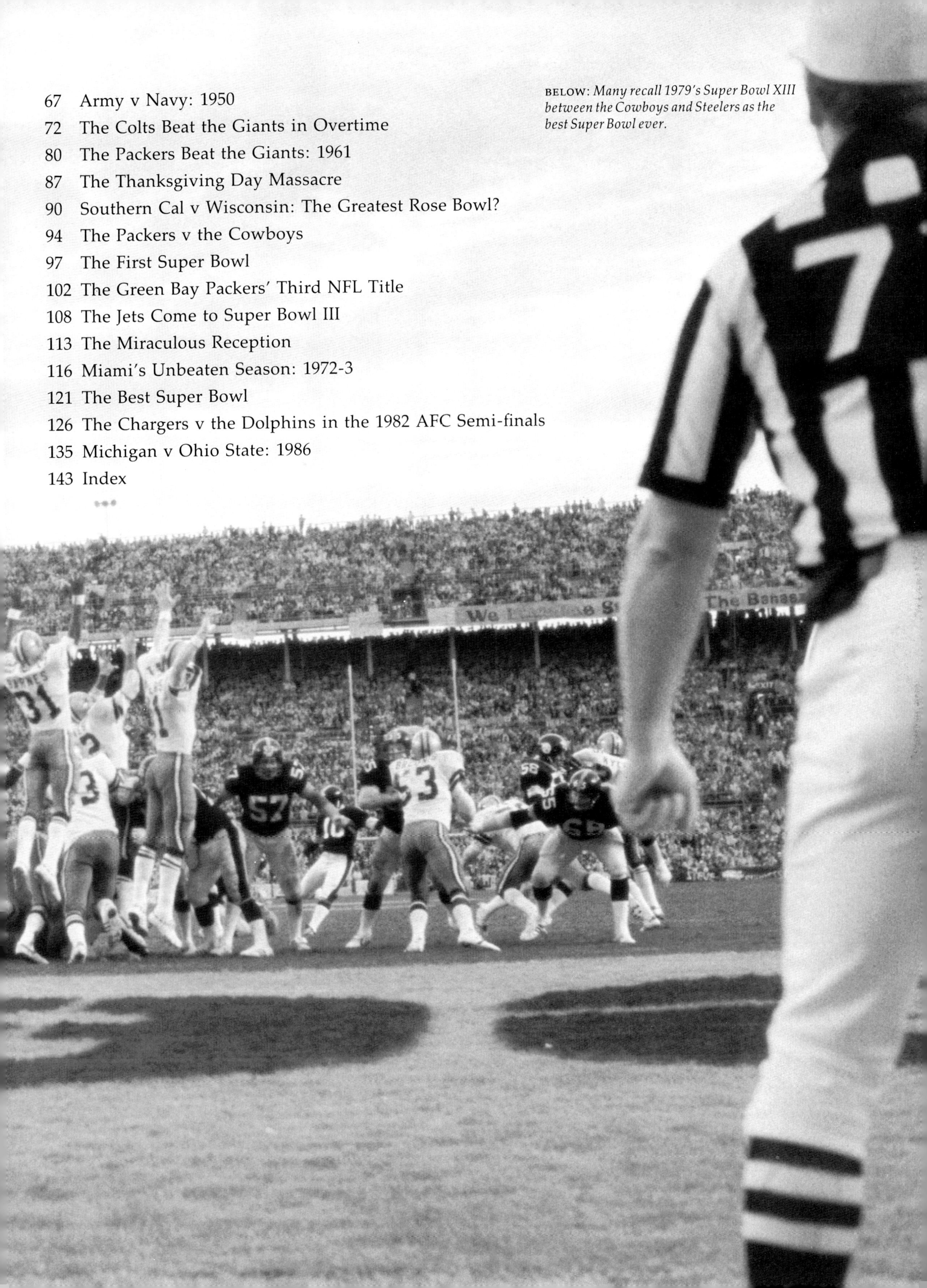

BELOW: *Many recall 1979's Super Bowl XIII between the Cowboys and Steelers as the best Super Bowl ever.*

INTRODUCTION

The first exhibition game of the 1986 National Football League was played between the defending champions, the Chicago Bears, and a perennial contender, the Dallas Cowboys. They did not meet in Soldier Field, the Bears' home, or in Texas Stadium, home of the Cowboys. Rather, the two teams crossed the Atlantic and exhibited America's brand of football in England.

It seems only fitting that the Bears and Cowboys should return to the land where football began. History tells us that for centuries, the Danes (or Norsemen or Vikings; it doesn't matter what you call them) would sail over to England and plunder, burn, loot, rape and generally misbehave. After centuries of having their country ravaged, the British found a hero. They called him King Alfred, and today he is referred to in the history books as Alfred the Great. He defeated the Danes at Ethandun (Eddington) around 890 AD, and during his reign Alfred developed many of the laws and systems that brought England out of the Dark Ages and made her the equal of her continental European rivals. Yet one creation for which Alfred the Great did not receive credit is football.

If you believe the legend-makers, after their victory at Ethandun the euphoric British decapitated all the Danish dead and took to kicking their heads about the battlefield. This quickly developed into a kind of gigantic soccer game without rules. The troops enjoyed this pastime so much that they continued the sport the next day. Alfred liked seeing his subjects have fun, but he knew that the supply of Danish heads was short, so he suggested to his chancellor that he find a substitute ball for the troops. Someone in the court remembered seeing one of the servants pour wine out of a pig bladder, and in a flash the first football was born.

To be sure, except for the bloodthirsty way in which they went about it, Alfred's troops hadn't quite invented football. But they had invented soccer, and although many kings subsequently tried to ban it, this

ABOVE and RIGHT: *By 1986 American football was an international sport. Thus the first NFL exhibition game of the season was played in England.*

LEFT: *Ancestor of modern football was the game invented at Rugby School in England.*

rowdy game gradually established itself as a national sport. Over the years the rules were refined, but the nature of the game itself didn't change until the nineteenth century.

In 1823, on the playingfield of Rugby School, an intramural soccer game was being played. One of the players was a young man named William Webb Ellis. Young Mr Ellis was not much of a soccer player, and every time the ball was bounced over to him, he'd take a good, hard kick at it, miss and land on his caudal. Annoyed both by the laughter of the other players and soreness of his posterior, Ellis decided to get even. The next time the ball came his way, Ellis picked it up and started running down the field. The other players looked on in horror as Ellis bolted toward the surprised goalie. The players, shocked by this breach of etiquette, took off after the radical. They caught him near the goal, jumped all over him and gave him a sound thrashing. Ellis's teammates then apologized to their opponents for his behavior, and he was thrown off the field.

But some who had seen Ellis's run thought he might have discovered something. Soon others at Rugby College joined Ellis in changing soccer's rules to permit players to pick up the ball and run with it. They began to have their own games, in which, to stop a runner, they tackled him. Since the runners had no blockers or protective equipment, the school infirmary was soon filled with students who played Ellis's game.

Purists looked down their noses at players who would use their hands to play soccer, and it took Ellis's game a long time to catch on in England, but when it did it became known as Rugby. The body contact of Rugby appealed to Americans, and when Harvard began playing what they called 'the Boston Game,'

Rugby quickly became accepted in the US.

Although the College Football Hall of Fame credits Princeton and Rutgers with having played the first intercollegiate football game in America, what they played that November afternoon in 1869 at New Brunswick, NJ, was a far cry from today's game. There were 25 players on each side, the ball was kicked or butted with the head and carrying the ball was forbidden. In fact, this first football game was nothing but a kind of soccer match (with Rutgers winning 6-4).

In 1873 a few Eastern universities met to form a football (*ie* soccer) league. Harvard refused to join, preferring instead to go on playing their 'Boston Game.' In 1874, McGill University in Montréal, Canada, challenged Harvard to a game. McGill played Rugby, to which the 'Boston game' was similar. The two sides soon ironed out the differences. Harvard agreed to adopt the running and tackling that Rugby called for, and McGill agreed to the kicking game that was a feature of 'Boston' football. Even though the Rugby rules dominated, the Harvardians proved to be as smart on the playing field as they were in the classroom. Harvard won the first game 3-0. The second was a 0-0 tie, and Harvard won the rubber match 3-0.

The next year Harvard challenged Yale to a game and college football's longest football rivalry began. Thus on 13 November 1875, on a neutral field at Hamilton Park in Springfield, MA, the first true American football game was played. Harvard won 4-0 and for the first time the players on each team wore uniformly colored jerseys. For the Yalies it was blue shirts and yellow caps. The Harvardians wore crimson shirts, with crimson pants and crimson stockings. It was colorful, memorable and the start of a fall madness that grips this country every year.

In the next few years the rules of American football really began to fall into place. In 1880 the 11-man team, with a seven-man rushing line, and the 110-yard field were made standard. (The 100-yard field, with end zones, was not finally adopted until 1912.) By 1882 the system of downs had been worked out, the field had been marked off in yard lines, plays were being called by means of signals and linemen were beginning to learn the art of blocking. Football was still mainly a kicking game, since a field goal counted five points, a kick after touchdown four points and a touchdown itself only two points. But in 1884 it was agreed that a touchdown should count four points and the kick after touchdown was reduced to two, thus beginning the process of changing football to a running game. (The kick after touchdown was reduced to one point in 1897; the field goal was reduced to three points in 1909; and the touchdown was raised to six points in 1912.)

Yale dominated football in the 1880s. In 1882 Yale outscored all its opponents 482-2; and in 1888, 698-0! And in 157-pound Walter Chauncey Camp, its star halfback in 1879, Yale produced a man who was to have a profound influence on the future of the game. Camp became Yale's athletic director in 1888 and was one of the guiding lights of the Intercollegiate Football Rules Committee for the next 48 years. As such he was personally responsible for formulating many – if not most – of the rules that both govern and define today's game. But almost as important was his role in bringing football to the attention of the American public. Beginning as a consultant to *The Week's Sports* and *Harper's Weekly*, he soon became the country's premier football journalist and was primarily responsible for picking the first 'All American' team (*ie* best players of the year) in 1889. By the turn of the century Camp's annual All American selections were so eagerly awaited by both the press and the public that he had to guard them like state secrets right up to the moment of publication. In the early decades of the

twentieth century Camp was popularly known as 'The Father of American Football,' and it is hard to think of anyone more deserving of the title.

In one respect, however, football hadn't changed much since the days of Alfred the Great. It was still probably the most brutal team sport played anywhere in the Western world. As players and coaches began to develop a better sense of tactics, they realized that certain massed formations – notably the infamous nine-man flying wedge – were practically unstoppable. Any defensive players who tried to 'bust' such big wedge formations were liable to get totalled. And that is not just a figure of speech. By the turn of the century about a half dozen players were being killed on football fields every year, and when the 1905 season ended, no less than 18 young men had died of football injuries and 160 more were on hospital critical lists.

Among the many who were appalled by this carnage was President Theodore Roosevelt. He summoned the presidents of Harvard, Yale and Princeton to his office and, declaring that 'brutality and foul play should receive the same summary punishment given to a man who cheats at cards,' threatened to bar football by executive order unless the colleges could find ways to clean up the game and make it safer.

ABOVE: *Walter Camp.*

LEFT: *Rutgers v Princeton, 1869. This 'first intercollegiate football game' would hardly be recognizable as football today.*

RIGHT: *The Yale-Princeton game of 1881 led Camp to invent the system of downs.*

BELOW: *The infamous flying wedge, soon to be banned, was nearly unstoppable.*

On 12 January 1906 a group that represented the football-playing colleges announced a sweeping new set of rules for the game. Massed formations were outlawed, as were a number of dangerous plays such as 'hurdling,' or trying to vault over players who were still standing. Before the start of each play the opposing lines had to be separated by a yard-wide neutral zone called the line of scrimmage. The total time of play was reduced to 60 minutes (90-minute games had previously been common), and a second referee was placed on the field. There were many other new rules, but one that was considered to be of little importance at the time ultimately proved to be an innovation of fundamental importance: The seldom-used 'trick' play known as the forward pass was declared legal.

Either despite or because of its violence, football had become immensely popular by the early years of the twentieth century. Harvard built a 30,000-seat concrete football stadium in 1903, and in the years that followed many other schools, such as Syracuse, Princeton and Yale, followed suit. The first 'million-dollar' stadium was built by Ohio State in the early 1920s, and by 1926 as many as 110,000 fans would be thronging into Chicago's newly-built Soldier Field to watch Army play Navy. From the outset it was expected that these huge, costly stadiums would justify themselves by showing a profit. And the fact that they *did* show profits made it inevitable that another kind of football – 'professional' football – would sooner or later appear on the scene.

In fact, small pro teams had been playing sporadically about the country since the early 1890s, and by 1922 the National Football League had been formed. But despite the fact that athletes of the caliber of the great Jim Thorpe were playing in the NFL, pro football hadn't really caught on with the public, largely because most people still felt that it lacked the cachet, the excitement and probably the honesty of college football. What pro ball needed was a national hero, and it found him in 1925 when the already-famous former halfback of the University of Illinois, Red Grange, signed with the Chicago Bears. Grange proved to be such an extraordinary box office draw that when the touring Bears played the financially faltering New York Giants in the Polo Grounds, some 70,000 paying fans turned out to witness the event, thereby probably saving the Giants' franchise. From that fabulous 1925 season on, professional football never had to look back.

Football had by now joined baseball as one of the nation's two favorite sports, and like baseball, it was rapidly beginning to manufacture not only heroes, but a whole body of popular lore and tradition. Famous inter-team rivalries developed, as did the many rituals associated with college homecoming games, pro championship games and the like. The Rose Bowl game began to be played on an annual basis in 1916, and by the end of the 1930s similar postseason games were being played in the Orange Bowl, the Sugar Bowl, the Sun Bowl and the Cotton Bowl. The annual All Star game between the NFL champions and the best college seniors was begun in 1934. The first pro Super Bowl Game was not played until 1967, and at the time it was neither a sellout nor a TV sensation, but in a few years it would become both

– would become, in fact, the subject of a kind of national mania. No less an authority than Dr Norman Vincent Peale was quoted by *Time* as saying of the 1981 game, 'If Jesus were alive today he would be at the Super Bowl.'

Since the turn of the century, when Fielding H Yost took his 'point-a-minute' Michigan Wolverines out to Pasadena, California, to defeat Stanford in the first Tournament of Roses Game in 1901, football, college and pro, has provided fans with some of the most memorable moments in sports. In fact, there have been so many memorable moments in football that it's almost impossible to name them all. And of course what constitutes a 'great' moment to some extent de-

ABOVE: *The formal dedication of Soldier Field in Chicago witnessed the 29th Army-Navy game, 27 November 1926.*
LEFT: *W A Roger's 1891 engraving 'Out of the Game' reflects the public perception of football as a game of unbridled violence.*

pends on your point of view. When Bart Starr scored on that 1967 quarterback sneak and gave the Green Bay Packers their third straight NFL title, the Dallas Cowboys and their fans fell into a pit of despair that not even Dante could describe. When Red Grange scored four touchdowns in the first 12 minutes of the 1925 Illinois game against Michigan, he ran into the record books and established himself as a charter member of the Golden Age of Sport, joining Babe Ruth, Jack Dempsey, Bobby Jones and Bill Tilden as gods in our sports pantheon. But alas, poor Michigan.

Sometimes a memorable moment occurs in just a few seconds, like Starr's sneak, or it can take a whole game, like the Giants-Colts 1958 NFL title game, often called the 'greatest game ever played.' It can be created by an individual like Grange or by a team of nobodies, like Columbia beating the great Army team in 1947.

Of all sports, football is the one where the coach is likely to be the most important person on a team. In baseball, the game is between pitcher and hitter, with the fielders as backup to the pitcher. A baseball manager may influence one or two games a season, but if the hitters don't hit or the pitcher doesn't pitch well, all the manager's knowledge isn't going to help. In basketball, especially at the professional level, the talent is so good that a coach's biggest problem is to get playing time for the stars on the bench. In college basketball, perhaps only John Wooden, Bobby Knight, Denny Crumm and Dean Smith have the records to show that their coaching makes a difference.

But in football, the coach is king. At the college level, especially nowadays, the coach is largely a recruiter, and if he gets the blue chip players coming out of high school, he'll be a winner (provided, of course, his recruits can stay in school). But at the professional level, where all the passers can throw a ball far and accurately, where all the runners are quick, fast and strong, where all the receivers are swift and sure-handed, and where all the defensive players are big, mean and talented, the difference between winners and losers is coaching. True football fans recognize this, and even though the players may seem the heroes of the moment, the fans know that the great teams in the history of football are always those created by great coaches. Inevitably, in a book such as this one, great coaches emerge as the real superstars.

If the unforgettable moments that football's finest coaches and players have given us over the years are too numerous to list; what hope is there of trying to describe them all in the pages of a single volume? The answer, of course, is none. For every moment included in this book there must be dozens of others, equally deserving, that have had to be left out for want of space. But then my purpose was never to write a history of football. Rather, this book is meant to be an evocation, an attempt to capture the unique spirit of this wonderful game by trying to create a representative few of its many great moments in words and pictures. If any readers think that I've succeeded in this, I'll be very pleased.

Notre Dame Upsets Army
1913

In 1913 the powerful West Point football team played a small Catholic college from South Bend, Indiana. It seems that the small school's coach, a man named Jess Harper, had written to the Commandant of the Corps of Cadets and asked if his school, Notre Dame, could play against Army at West Point. The Commandant had barely heard of the school, and he was about to throw the letter away when he decided to pass it on to the Army football coach as a joke. But when the coach received the letter, he didn't laugh. He had heard of Notre Dame and knew that they were pretty good. So he wrote Jess Harper, and they scheduled the game for 1 November 1913.

For the Notre Dame team, the game against Army was their biggest challenge ever. The entire student body came down to the train station to see the team board the day coach from South Bend to Buffalo. Each player was burning with the desire to prove that Notre Dame was as good a team as any in the country. As Knute Rockne later wrote 'We went out to play Army like crusaders, believing that we represented not only our own school but the whole aspiring Middle West.'

Most Army fans regarded the game with Notre Dame as little more than a good workout for the powerful Cadets, and when the Notre Dame team came on the field they were sure of it. Only 18 players represented the small school, while Army had 50 or more on the sidelines. Army, typical of football teams of that day, was a heavyweight team, with large linemen blocking for strong, hard runners. On average they outweighed the Notre Dame team by 25 pounds a man, and the writers covering the game for the New York and other Eastern papers considered the whole thing to be a hopeless mismatch.

And in the first quarter, they seemed to be correct. The Cadets marched down the field and used the pass to get into scoring position for the first touchdown. The passing combination of Vernon Prichard to John Jouett also set up a second Army touchdown, and they had a commanding 13-0 lead. But going in for a third score, Prichard's pass was picked off in the end zone by Charles Dorais of Notre Dame.

Knute Kenneth Rockne, Notre Dame's great head coach, 1918-31. His amazing record: 105 wins, 12 defeats and five ties.

And now Notre Dame took over. All summer long, Charles 'Gus' Dorais and his friend and teammate, Knute Rockne, had practiced passing and catching the ball on the shores of Lake Erie, where they held summer jobs as waiters in a restaurant. Rockne would run precise patterns in the sand, and Dorais would pass the ball to him, throwing to a spot where he knew Rockne would be. Over and over, day after day, Rockne would run his patterns, and Dorais would deliver the ball. At that time the passing game was basically one in which a receiver would run as fast as he could down the field, and the passer would try to throw the ball so that the receiver could run under it. Rockne worked on short 'out' patterns, 'hook' patterns and 'post' patterns, as well as deep passes, while Dorais worked on his delivery, throwing hard, quick passes on the short routes and lofting the ball on the longer passes. Going into the Army game, Notre Dame had won three games in a row by a total of 169 points to seven for the opposition. So whatever else it might be, this was a team that could score.

From the second quarter on, the team from that small town in Indiana dominated Army as no team had ever done to the Black Knights of the Hudson. Gus Dorais, a small 145-pound passer and runner, drove the big Army lineman crazy. They couldn't catch him when they rushed, and if they tried to contain him, he just flipped one of his passes to Rockne or Fred Gushurst, the other end, or to his backs coming out of the backfield.

After the interception, the Irish had driven the length of the field, combining passes with runs. Army fans and the Eastern writers covering the game couldn't believe their eyes. Twice Notre Dame scored in the second quarter and led at halftime 14-13.

When the third quarter started, Army changed its defense to give greater coverage to the Notre Dame receivers. Dorais outfoxed them and had his runners darting through and around the spread-out Army defenders. Then, when Army tightened up to stop the running, Dorais and the receivers combined to pass Army silly.

Rockne came out of a pile-up limping, a fact that the Army defender guarding him noticed. Dorais threw three passes to Joe Piska, and after each completion Rockne hobbled back to the huddle. The third time Rockne ran his pattern, the Army defender ignored him and helped out on the other Irish receiver. With the ball on the Army 40, Dorais and Rockne sprang the trap. Dorais took the snap from the center and rolled to his left, looking at Gushurst. Rockne limped down field, and when the Army defender ignored him, he took off. Dorais stopped, turned and threw the ball deep across the field, and Rockne ran under it, catching the pass on the Army five and scoring. The rout was complete. Notre Dame-35, Army-13.

All in all, Dorais threw 17 passes, an amazing number for those days, and he completed 14, for a completion percentage of .82, an astounding figure even today.

All five Notre Dame touchdowns came via the pass, and the press made sure that the football world knew about this new kind of football. To be sure, the forward pass had been used before, but the way Notre Dame passed made all former uses look like playing with a medicine ball.

The great Notre Dame victory made the little school the talk of the sports world, and the forward pass quickly became part of the offensive repertoire of almost every team in the country. Coaches from all levels wrote to Notre Dame for instructions on how to install a passing offense. The Neanderthal days of football were over, and the names of Gus Dorais, Knute Rockne and Notre Dame will forever be linked with the dawn of the new era.

After the game Notre Dame coach Jess Harper dropped into the office of Army coach Charley Daly to express his appreciation for Army's scheduling of Notre Dame. There were some Army brass there, and Harper noticed one general angrily berating his wife.

'Well?' the general said. 'You're the one that's been hollering about how we don't play any decent opposition. Now, dammit, are you satisfied?'

BELOW LEFT: *Rockne before the 1913 game with Army in which he and Dorais first used the newfangled forward pass.*

BELOW RIGHT: *Charles E 'Gus' Dorais was the passing half of the Rockne-Dorais combo that changed football forever.*

JIM THORPE and the beginnings of pro football

For years, long before there was a National Football League, college boys had been picking up extra money by playing with semi-pro teams in their areas. The teams they played with were usually sponsored by some factory in a town or by the town itself. Rockne, Dorais and George Gipp did this, and so did Pudge Heffelfinger, the great All American from Yale. In fact, records suggest that Heffelfinger may have been the first paid player in football history. In the archives of the Professional Football Hall of Fame in Canton, Ohio, a yellowed financial statement carries the entry, 'Pudge Heffelfinger, $500 (for playing).' He was playing for a team in Pittsburgh against another Pittsburgh club team.

In those days it wasn't unusual for a college star to go to another town and play on Sunday for a few bucks, and it wasn't unheard of if that same player played for different teams. Knute Rockne, while at Notre Dame, played for at least six different teams in one season in 1915.

Most of the pro or semi-pro teams were located in the industrial belt of the country, and many of the clubs were financially supported by steel mills, oil companies, railroads or coal mines. The owners of those companies knew that their employees worked under tough conditions for poor wages, and they also knew that a good, hard-hitting football game could be an outlet for their workers that would be both welcome and inexpensive. The names of the teams reflected the game itself – basic, hard-hitting and physical. There were, for example, the Providence Steamrollers, The Massillon Tigers, the Canton Bulldogs and the Columbus Panhandles. Towns with teams challenged their neighbors, and if they couldn't get enough players from the factories and the coal fields, they brought in college players and paid them.

In 1913, the most famous athlete in the world signed to play football for a fee, and now, for the first time, major newspapers began to take notice of the pros. The athlete's name was Jim Thorpe, and in the 1912 Olympic Games in Stockholm, Sweden, this Sac & Fox Indian had won both the decathlon and the pentathlon. When the King of Sweden presented Thorpe with his gold medal, he said 'Sir, you are the greatest athlete who ever lived.' He was probably right.

When Jim Thorpe came home after his personal triumphs, he found that there was little in terms of monetary reward for a man who could throw the discus and run the mile. So he sold his enormous talents to the highest bidder, a football team in Pine Valley, Pennsylvania, where he would play for 12 years. Those who played with or against him always called him 'Big Jim.' By today's standards, he probably wouldn't be allowed on a college team. He stood six feet tall but weighed only about 175 pounds. But that didn't measure his heart. He was easily the best all-round football player of his time. He could drop kick over 50 yards, pass, catch and play defense, but what he was best at was running the ball. When Thorpe was carrying he was a dangerous man to try to tackle. Thorpe would shift his hip towards the tackler as he approached, then he'd take it away. As the tackler made contact, Thorpe would throw that hip into the head of the tackler and leave him for dead on the turf. Old timers who saw Thorpe play say he ran with the abandon of a Jimmy Taylor. Fans filled the small grandstands in the towns when Thorpe and whatever team he was playing with visited town.

ABOVE: *The Massillon Tigers of 1919. In the season's showdown game the Canton Bulldogs beat them 3-0 on a Jim Thorpe fieldgoal.*

He once even formed his own team, the Oorang Indians, and recruited many of his old teammates from the Carlisle Indian Industrial School. He had special shoulder pads made for himself, and George Halas swore they were made of sheet metal. Over the years he played with and against the greatest players of his day, and on the strength of his name and ability, Jim Thorpe, almost single-handed, carried pro football into the Roaring Twenties and gave it a chance to stay alive.

The team with which Thorpe made his football reputation was the Canton (Ohio) Bulldogs. When he signed with them in 1915 he had previously played only one full season of pro ball, and not a particularly memorable season, at that. But the ink was hardly dry on his $250-per-game contract when he was plunged into a two-game series with

LEFT: *James Francis Thorpe in the uniform of the Carlisle (PA) Indian School, 1909. He was not, in fact, a full-blooded Indian.*

RIGHT: *William 'Pudge' Heffelfinger, Yale's great guard (1888-91), may have been the first paid pro star.*

BELOW: *This old photo not withstanding, the Bulldogs in 1920 ranked third after the Akron Pros and Decatur Staleys.*

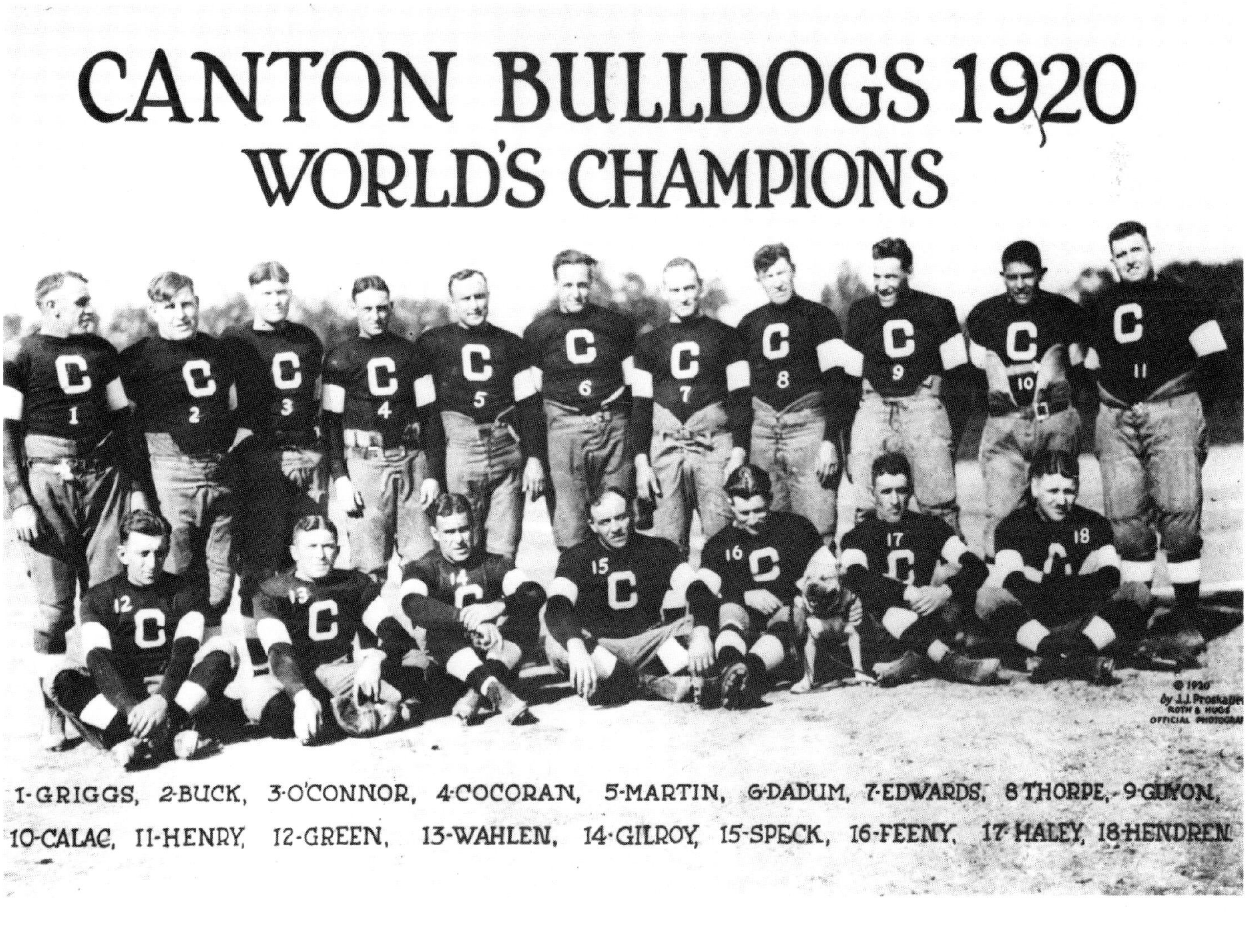

the Bulldog's chief rivals, the Massillon Tigers. The Bulldogs lost the first game and won the second, but what everyone remembered about that second game was *how* the Bulldogs won. Nothing could have summed up better the boisterous free-for-all nature of early pro football.

Going into the third quarter the Bulldogs led 6-0, thanks to two dropkicked fieldgoals by Thorpe. But then a Massillon end caught a pass on the Bulldog's 15 and, hotly pursued by Canton's Charley Smith, dashed into the end zone and vanished into the milling throng of spectators crowded there. Since the possibility of this kind of disappearing act had been foreseen, the teams had agreed beforehand that anyone who was lost from sight after crossing a goal line still had to be in possession of the ball when he emerged from the crowd. But in this case, when the two players came back on the field, it wasn't the Massillon end who had the ball; it was Smith!

No one could figure out what had happened. The referee tried to rule the play a touchback, rather than a touchdown, but by now the field was in such a state of riot that the game had to be called. Later that evening the officials met and, after some debate, upheld the referee's call, thus awarding the game to Canton on the basis of the lead established by Thorpe's two goals. Only years later did the truth come out. In the dense, shoving crowd in the Canton end zone one of the spectators – a trolley-car conductor – had kicked the ball out of the Massillon player's hand, and somehow it had landed in the arms of the startled Smith, who then carried it triumphantly back on to the field.

If Smith, Thorpe, or any of the other Bulldogs ever felt that there was something fishy about how Smith got the ball, they never let on. In the world of pro football in 1915 you won any way you could, and nobody was more dedicated to winning than the Bulldogs. They proved that the following year – one of Thorpe's best – by winning 10 straight and becoming the pro football champions of the world.

Although historians agree that it was during his years with the Bulldogs that Thorpe played his greatest football, it is almost impossible to cite chapter and verse. There are tantalizing tales of 90-yard punts and 75-yard fieldgoals, but we shall never really know, for in those boisterous years of pro football's infancy nobody kept official records.

Towards the end of his career, playing for the Toledo Maroons, Thorpe

LEFT: *Thorpe excelled in punting.*

ABOVE: *Thorpe (20) of the Bulldogs downs a player of the Buffalo All Americans in a 1920 game played in the Polo Grounds.*

LEFT: *Jim Thorpe: A 1950 Associated Press poll rated him the century's finest athlete, far ahead, even, of Babe Ruth.*

played against a team called the Oklahoma All Stars. They were led by a great tackle named Steve Owen. Twice Owen ran over Thorpe to tackle the ball carrier. Owen told the teammate beside him, 'Old Jim's slowed up. He doesn't like to block anymore.' On the next play Thorpe creamed Owen with a vicious, bone-breaking block. As the astonished Owen groggily got to his feet, Thorpe winked at him and said, 'Always keep an eye on an old Indian, son.'

Big Jim ended his career with the New York Giants in 1925. By then he was a ghost of the Jim Thorpe who had been the world's greatest athlete. The years of pounding and being pounded, the booze, the late nights and the wild times had taken their toll. But even as his career was ending, a red-headed legend named Grange was getting ready to bring Thorpe's game into the major leagues. Pro football owed a great deal to the men who played for the steel mills and the coal towns and the farm villages of this country and kept the game alive. But most of all it owed a debt to Jim Thorpe, the player whom the people paid to watch.

THE FOUR HORSEMEN

Since that October day in 1913 when Gus Dorais and Knute Rockne passed Army silly on the plains of West Point, the game between Notre Dame and Army had become a national event. The stadiums at the two schools were too small to hold the thousands of people who wanted to see the game, so both schools agreed that they would play in New York, in the Polo Grounds. The team Knute Rockne brought to Gotham in 1924 was considered one of the nation's best. The Army team opposing them was rated even higher.

College football in 1924 was filling stadiums nationwide. Each section of the country claimed to have the top teams. Army, Yale, Harvard, Princeton and Navy in the East, Georgia Tech, Alabama, Duke and Texas in the South, and Stanford and USC in the West, all claimed to be the Nation's best. But in truth, most of the best teams in the country that year were in the Middle West. Red Grange of Illinois was already an All American, and at Michigan they were comparing the 1924 Wolverines with the best teams Fielding H Yost had ever produced. In the end it all came down to four teams: Michigan, Illinois, Army and Notre Dame. Since Army was scheduled to

LEFT: *Quarterback Stuhldreher was the play-caller and main passer of the Horsemen.*

RIGHT: *In the 1924 Rose Bowl not even Ernie Nevers, Stanford's star QB, who gained 114 yards in 34 plays, could stop the Irish.*

BELOW: *Fullback Elmer Layden, the Horsemen's best defensive player. He would later coach at Notre Dame.*

LEFT TOP: *Knute Rockne became Notre Dame's head coach in 1918. The next year saw his first all-victorious season, in which his team won nine straight.*

LEFT BELOW: *The famous publicity shot of The Four Horsemen mounted. Left to right: Don Miller, Elmer Layden, Jim Crowley and Harry Stuhldreher.*

play Notre Dame on 18 October and Illinois was playing Michigan the next day, the conflict between Army and Notre Dame promised to be the opening act of two days of some of the best college football in history.

When the first game ended, the score read Notre Dame-13, Army-7. It had been a hard-fought game, but the speed and grace of the Notre Dame team led the most famous and beloved sports writer of all time to pen an inspired lead.

'Outlined against the blue-grey October sky, The Four Horsemen rode again. In dramatic lore they are known as famine, pestilence, destruction and death. These are only aliases. Their real names are Stuhldreher, Miller, Crowley and Layden.' So wrote Grantland Rice in his column reporting the game, and when some enterprising publicity man for Notre Dame read Rice's lines, he had the four players photographed dressed in their football uniforms and mounted on horses. Thus the most famous backfield combination in history was born.

Nothing before in football had so captured the public's imagination, and soon Notre Dame games were sellouts wherever the Irish played. They were an ideal school for the publicity mills. Their coach, Knute Rockne, was witty, charming, bright and the best coach in the business. His teams were quick and speedy, giving football a wide open look that sharply contrasted with the plodding formations of the opposition. And the Four Horsemen themselves were the kind of young men that every mother would want her daughter to marry.

Harry Stuhldreher was Rockne's quarterback and field general. He handled the play-calling and passing and was a great blocker. He would later become a most successful coach at the University of Wisconsin. Don Miller was very fast and the best broken field runner of the group. The left halfback was Jim Crowley, nicknamed 'Sleepy Jim', their best all-round back. He would eventually go to Fordham, where he would coach the famed Seven Blocks of Granite and a young guard named Vince Lombardi. The fullback was Elmer Layden, the most serious of the group and the best defensive player in the backfield. Layden would return to Notre Dame in the 1930s to coach the Irish.

Modern high schools have heavier backfields than the Four Horsemen: Their average weight was only about 160 pounds. But they had speed, agility and surprising strength. They ran and slashed their way across the country, and when the 1924 season ended, they were undefeated. The only team in the country that the experts said could beat Notre Dame was the Stanford Indians, led by their great fullback, Ernie Nevers.

Rockne and the Irish accepted the invitation to play the Indians in the Rose Bowl, and the game lived up to all hopes. Nevers was great, and the Stanford team was magnificent, yet the Irish prevailed. Elmer Layden intercepted two Stanford passes and returned them for touchdowns. The 200-pound Nevers hammered the smaller Irish line, but late in the third quarter, on fourth down with inches to go for a score, the Irish rose up and stopped the great runner on the eight-inch line!

Some 52,000 people had filled the Rose Bowl to see the Four Horsemen against Ernie Nevers, the largest crowd so far in Rose Bowl history. When it was over they saw the Four Horsemen ride off into the sunset of football immortality.

The Galloping Ghost

During the football season of 1922 word spread through the football world that there was a back on the freshman team at the University of Illinois who would someday be a star. The scouts who had visited the Champaign campus returned to their schools with rave notices about the young man, but even their most lavish praise fell short of the mark.

From the first game Harold 'Red' Grange played at Illinois in 1923, until his last in 1925, he was without question the greatest running back football ever saw. They called him the Galloping Ghost, and Grantland Rice wrote a poem about Grange that came as close as anybody trying to describe the wonderful redhead.

A streak of fire, a breath of flame,
Eluding all who reach and clutch
A gray ghost thrown into the game
That rivals' hands may never
touch . . .

As the exploits of Grange were reported to avid listeners and readers across the country, Grange became the most famous player in football history. Only the Four Horsemen and Notre Dame could rival him in terms of publicity, and the public could not get enough of him. They tried to nominate him for Congress and named towns after him. They even went to see the embarrassing and forgettable Western that Hollywood persuaded him to make.

Still, there were a few who persisted in doubting that anyone could be that good. One of the doubters was Fielding H Yost, the legendary coach of the powerful Michigan Wolverines, for from 1921 through the early part of the 1924 season Yost's team had been undefeated. The schedule-makers in the Big Ten had marked 19 October as the date when Illinois and Michigan would play. The game would be played at Champaign, where the Illini were to dedicate their new 66,000-seat stadium.

Early in the season, Yost had been asked by a writer what he thought of Red Grange. Dismissively, Yost replied, 'All Grange can do is run.' When Bob Zuppke, the Illinois coach, was asked to comment on Yost's remark, he snapped 'Yes, and all Galli-Curci can do is sing.'

When the two teams met that fall afternoon, the Illinois press box was filled with writers from the East and West, many of whom had only read about the Ghost, since the Illini didn't travel beyond the Big Ten stadiums. But one thing they knew, if only from the record books, was that the Michigan team facing Grange and his teammates was one of the best in the country, for they hadn't lost a game in three years. They knew, too, that thousands of Michigan fans had driven or trailed down from Ann Arbor to see Illinois. What they couldn't know was that they were about to see what was without

question the single greatest performance by a running back in the history of the game, and that includes *every* running back, past and present.

Illinois won the toss and elected to receive. Michigan kicked off. Grange was the only man back for Illinois, and the ball bounced in front of him on his own five. He caught it on the first bounce and headed straight up the field. As the first wave of Michigan men met Grange's blockers, Grange cut to his right and broke through the first line of defenders. Now the Michigan team tried to force him towards the sidelines, and as they converged on Grange, he slowed and began drifting to his left, and as the Michigan players ran past him, he accelerated, cutting diagonally left and then heading on up the field. Now the first wave of Wolverines was back in pursuit of Grange, but

ABOVE: *Harold Edward 'Red' Grange, probably history's greatest broken-field runner. He gained 4280 yards in three years playing for Illinois, 3637 of them by rushing.*

ABOVE LEFT: *Grange on a touchdown run in the 1924 Michigan game, the high point of his college playing career. He scored five of Illinois's six touchdowns rushing, and it was on his 23-yard pass that the sixth was made. Illinois won by 25 points.*

he kept ahead of them, and, passing midfield, he had only two Michigan men before him. He feinted as if he were going straight up field, and as the nearer Michigan man moved, Grange shifted to his left and was past him. The rest was a foot race, and when it was over, Grange stood in the Michigan end zone and touched the ball down. Illinois-6, Michigan-0. The stadium was rocking as Grange's teammates pounded him on the back. The run had taken all of 10 seconds and the extra point was good.

Michigan was stopped cold on its first offensive drive and kicked to Grange. He caught the ball on his own 33 and headed upfield as the Michigan pursuit closed in. At the 40 Grange cut to his left and sprinted up the sidelines. At the Michigan 40 the Wolverines seemed to have him pinned on the sideline at last, but suddenly Grange cut to his right and headed for the center of the field. At the 30 he cut back to his left, directly counter to the course his pursuers were on, and before the Michigan team could recover, Grange was standing in the Michigan end zone. With the extra point made, the score was Illinois-14, Michigan-0, and Fielding H Yost was finding remarkably little consolation in the thought that all Grange could do was run.

Again Michigan is stopped and forced to punt. This time, the punt is downed on the Illinois 44-yard line, and the Michigan fans experience a flicker of hope. Now that Grange isn't running in an open field, maybe the great Wolverine defense can turn the game around. Operating out of the single wing, the Illini snap the ball to their redheaded tailback. This time Grange and his blockers sweep to the right side, and the Illini linemen make their blocks to spring Grange into the clear at the 50. He turns upfield and simply outruns the rest of the Michigan players. With the extra point, it is Illinois-21, Michigan-0.

There are still seven minutes on the clock in the first quarter as the Illini kick off to Michigan. Their return gets them to their 28, and they know they have to score. But the Illinois defenders, the same players who were on offense, are not about to let Michigan back into the game. They shut down the Wolverines and force a punt. The Wolverine kicker has seen enough of Grange, so he kicks away with the ball, going out in Illinois territory.

With the ball on the Michigan 45, Grange sweeps to his left and then cuts back against the pursuit. At the Michigan 20, he weaves into his patented 'S' running style, cutting back to the left and speeding once more into the Michigan end zone. As he gives the ball to the referee, Grange glances up at the stadium clock. There are still three minutes left in the first quarter.

The new stadium is getting a real test of its strength as 66,000 fans roar and cheer. Bob Zuppke, standing on the sidelines, sends in a substitute for Grange before the extra point is kicked. When Grange comes to the sidelines the roar of the crowd makes it almost impossible for Zuppke to hear his question.

Grange, shouting: 'Why did you take me out?'

Zuppke, shouting: 'Not a Michigan man has touched you yet, and I wanted you to come out untouched.'

In the second half, Grange shows Yost he can do more than run. After scoring his fifth touchdown running, he passes 23 yards for the Illini sixth score. And whenever the Illinois team is kicking extra points or fieldgoals, the holder is Red Grange. The final score: 39-14.

When news of this fabulous game spread across the country, every team in America wanted to play Grange and the Illini. If Illinois had wanted, they could have played every day of each week in the year. And this public thirst to see the Galloping Ghost was not lost on promoters. Among those most interested were a man named C C Pyle and another named George Halas.

ABOVE: *Grange and Illinois coach Bob Zuppke. 'I will never have another Grange,' said Zup, 'but neither will anyone else.'*

BELOW: *Prior to the 1924 game Michigan's great coach, Fielding H Yost, said unwarily that 'all Grange can do is run.'*

GRANGE SIGNS WITH THE CHICAGO BEARS

When Red Grange announced after his last college game that he was going to turn pro and join the Chicago Bears, the news created a furor in intercollegiate sports. College presidents, coaches and alumni were outraged by the thought that their greatest player would join those Neanderthals who played football for pay. The Bears, their owner, George Halas and the National Football League were all attacked in virtually every paper in the country for tempting a college boy with the promise of money.

When Grange arrived in Chicago to sign formally with the Bears, the waiting room at Union Station was so crowded with promoters and agents trying to get Grange to sign something or other that there was no room for the passengers trying to catch their trains. Movie producers, book publishers, newspaper syndicators and many others were prepared to pay astronomical prices to put Grange under contract, but one man, a promoter from Champaign, Illinois, named CC ('Cash and Carry') Pyle, already had the most valuable contract of all. Grange had signed a personal services contract with Pyle – had in effect made him his manager – and Pyle in turn had negotiated the star's contract with George Halas.

Halas, himself a graduate of Illinois, knew that if pro football was ever going to compete for the public's dollar, it had to shed the image of a beer-bellied, dirty fighting, low-class game. And Halas also knew that there was probably only one man in America who could change that image.

When C C Pyle and Halas emerged from their meeting they announced that the Chicago Bears would play eight games in 12 days, starting in Chicago on Thanksgiving Day. When details of the Grange-Bears agreement finally reached the public, it made the Bears seem like a supporting cast for Caruso. Grange would be paid a percentage of the gate, with his percentage rising as more people paid to see him and the Bears. While at the time, Halas may have felt that these were harsh terms, whatever he paid Grange in 1925 would turn out to be the biggest bargain in pro football history.

BELOW: *Grange signs with the Chicago Bears. Left to right: Bears owner George Halas, Grange and Grange's manager, C C Pyle.*

In his first appearance as a professional football player Red Grange drew 35,000 people to Wrigley Field for a game against the Chicago Cardinals. The Bears made more money on that game than they had ever made. (And, of course, Grange did very well, thank you.) On to St Louis, then Philadelphia and, finally, New York.

In New York, the Bears were to face a new team in the National Football League. Earlier in the year, a respected bookmaker named Tim Mara was heading for the office of Billy Gibson to buy an interest in a young heavyweight contender named Gene Tunney. Mara ran into Joe Carr, the president of the NFL. Carr was also seeing Gibson, trying to interest him in buying and building a franchise in New York as part of the NFL. Gibson had turned Carr down.

'How much is a franchise worth?' asked Mara.

'Five hundred dollars,' responded Carr.

'Hell, any New York franchise is worth five hundred,' said Mara, taking out his checkbook and buying the franchise on the spot.

ABOVE: *Grange carries in the Bears-Giants game in New York, the most publicized pro game of 1925 – and in history, thus far.*

BELOW: *Tim Mara, owner of the NY Giants. Grange's appearance in the Giants-Bears game probably saved Mara's franchise.*

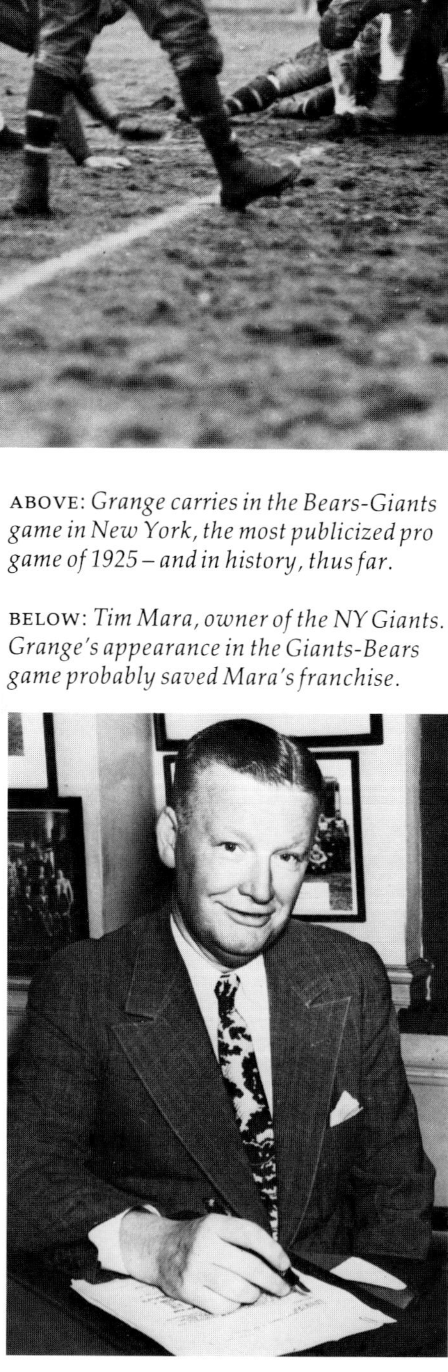

He decided to call his team the New York Football Giants. By the time the season was over, the Giants had been successful on the field but a box office turkey. Mara was already about $40,000 in the hole and decided to try and sign Red Grange for the next season. But Halas had already locked Grange up, so Mara did the next best thing and made a deal with Halas and Grange for a game in New York. He hoped that Grange would fill the Polo Grounds, so he printed up 70,000 tickets, and when the game was announced in the papers, the Giants' office was so flooded with requests that Tim Mara knew his first season as a pro football owner would be a success.

When Grange and the Bears walked out on the Polo Grounds field, the stadium was decorated as if a political convention were taking place. One goal was covered with gold and blue bunting for the Bears and the other with red and blue for the Giants. There were red, white and blue flags draped around the grandstand, and orange and blue around the bleachers. Around the edges of the field there were about 5000 fans, most of whom had climbed the bleachers or crashed the gate when all the tickets were sold. No accurate count was ever reached, but the best estimate of total attendance is that it was in excess of 70,000.

The game satisfied everyone. The New York fans cheered for Grange when the Bears had the ball and for the Giants when they had the ball. Because the field was muddy from two days of rain, there wasn't much chance for Grange to put on one of his great runs, so he simply ran up the middle on traps and off-tackle rushes or passed. When Grange sat down in the third quarter, the fans' interest in the game fell noticeably, but when he came back in the fourth, the Polo Grounds rocked, for Grange finally gave the fans the moment they had been hoping for.

Late in the game, with the Bears holding a short 12-7 lead, they had driven deep into Giants territory, with Grange leading the way. But the Giants stiffened and stopped Grange short of the goal. The Giants had been doing a lot of successful passing, and now again they took to the air. A pass downfield was complete, and the next one was fired to the sidelines. Just as it was about to be gathered in by the Giants' receiver, a player flashed in front and intercepted. The 70,000 rose as one as the Galloping Ghost sped down the sidelines, cut across the Giants' pursuit, dodged two tacklers near the five and raced into the end zone. The huge crowd roared: This was what they had paid to see. Red Grange had lived up to all of his billing.

The Bears and Grange made a tour of the South and the West, filling stadiums wherever they played. For three months, pro football monopolized the sports pages of the nation's newspapers. No longer would pro teams have to pass the hat to pay their players. The fields they would play on would be grass, the stadiums would be steel and concrete and they would be located in the major cities of the nation. Gone were the days of the company team and the high school field, the small towns and backwaters of football. No longer would pro football be a matter of pick-up teams from the local mills and college kids earning a couple of bucks by playing under assumed names. From now on it would be a major sport, all because of Red Grange.

RIGHT: *Grange and George Halas. The Bears' owner had, like Grange, played (1915-17) under Bob Zuppke at Illinois.*

BELOW: *The Chicago Bears in 1925. George Halas, who played end, is in the front row, far left. Grange is in the backfield, standing on the far right.*

The Giants beat the Bears in sneakers

The uproar that the colleges and universities raised when the Bears signed Red Grange prompted the NFL to come up with a rule that still exists. No pro team could sign a college player before his class was graduated. The player himself didn't have to be a graduate, but when his senior year was up and the graduation ceremonies were finished, the young men who had already made their fame on the gridiron could continue to play if they were good enough. This 'Graduation Rule' did much to alleviate the animosity the colleges felt towards the pros.

There still were too many teams in pro football (22), and they were a weird conglomeration. In addition to teams as professional as the Bears, Giants and Packers there were many teams as amateur as those of Hammond, Indiana, and Louisville, Kentucky – both of which played only four games, losing all, and then dropped out of the league.

In a meeting in 1927 the league decided to cut its membership from 22 teams to 10. By 1932, Pottsville, Duluth, Providence and several other smaller towns had also disappeared. (Providence had actually won the title in 1928, but when the Great Depression hit the country it was almost impossible to keep such franchises afloat). The explosion of interest in pro football that Red Grange had ignited seemed to have cooled to a dull ember. Something had to be done.

In July 1932 a man received a franchise in Boston. His name was George Preston Marshall, a man with style, an ego as big as any promoter in sports and an uncanny ability to see what pro football needed to compete with the college game. In 1933, at the league meetings, Marshall and George Halas pushed through two major rule changes. First, they got the league to agree to allow the passer to throw from

LEFT: *George Preston Marshall, owner of a laundry chain and football's Boston Braves.*

RIGHT: *In ex-Minnesota star 'Bronco' Nagurski the Bears found a ball carrier who 'ran his own interference.'*

BELOW: *One of many small franchises done in by the Depression was the Providence Steamrollers, NFL champions in 1928.*

anywhere behind the line of scrimmage. (Before, the passer had had to be at least five yards behind the line.) Second, Marshall and Halas got the league to break with tradition and move the goal posts ten yards closer to the goal line. The result was a faster, more open game, with increased scoring. And this, in turn, made it much more exciting and entertaining for the spectators.

Then Marshall made one more important proposal. He thought that, to increase interest, the NFL should emulate baseball and have two leagues, leading to a championship game between the league winners for a World Championship. Marshall insisted, and Halas agreed, that there should be a standard schedule, so that every team would play the same number of games against the same opponents. For the most part, everything that the flamboyant showman wanted – and got – is how the NFL operates today.

Among the benefits that Red Grange brought to the Chicago Bears, besides putting the Bears in the black, was that most of the college stars who wanted to play pro ball now wanted to play for the Bears. One of those young men was an All American fullback and tackle from Minnesota named Bronco Nagurski, and like Jim Thorpe and Red Grange before him, he came into the pros already a legend.

His name sounded like football, and he looked like football. He was broad-shouldered, had a scarred face, and with his massive thighs he could carry two or three tacklers into the end zone. Somber, tough and talented, Nagurski was surprisingly agile and quick for such a big man. Like all the players of the day he played both phases of the game, fullback on offense and tackle on defense. Because Nagurski was so powerful, the opposition always had to bunch up at the line of scrimmage to stop him. George Halas, the coach and owner of the Bears, recognized this and put in a special play for Nagurski. When the ball was centered to him, Nagurski would drive towards the line, and just as he got to the line and the defenders were closing in on him, Nagurski would stop and throw a short pass over the heads of the defenders to a Bears receiver cutting across the middle. In the Championship Game in 1933 against the New York Giants, Nagurski threw two touchdown passes with this play. The defenders were thoroughly confused. If they bunched to stop his line plunges, he'd pass over them. If they looked for the pass,

ABOVE: *Ken Strong, the Giants' ace kicker, making his 38-yard fieldgoal in the first quarter of the 1934 Giants-Bears game.*

RIGHT: *Giants quarterback Ed Danowski, one of the heroes of the 'Sneaker Game,' downs an onrushing Bronco Nagurski.*

Nagurski would be through the line and into the secondary, where his power and strength made it almost impossible to bring him down. The threat of his short passes may have been daunting, but when you think of Bronco Nagurski, you really think of power running, of a ball carrier bursting through a horde of tacklers, maybe carrying some on his back and leaving the rest strewn all over the field. To this day, Bronco Nagurski more perfectly fits the powerhouse image of a Chicago Bear than any player in that team's history.

The NFL's two-division arrangement had been in effect since 1933, when the Bears had beaten the Giants in Wrigley Field in Chicago. Over 30,000 spectators had attended. The Giants had lost the game to a Nagurski trick pass, and they had vowed revenge. In the 1934 season, both teams again won in their divisions and met on 10 December 1934 for the third NFL title game under the new division rule. (The Bears had won the first title game against Portsmouth in 1932.) To a man, the Giants knew they had to stop Nagurski, but their chances seemed very slim when they awoke that Sunday morning. Bitter cold gripped New York, and when the players came out on the field at the Polo Grounds the turf was already frozen. The Bears were delighted, because they thought the great Nagurski would be almost unstoppable if the Giants' tacklers couldn't get their footing.

Yet in the first quarter it was the Giants who seemed to have the edge. They moved downfield against the Bears, and Ken Strong, the great Giants fieldgoal kicker and defender kicked a 38-yarder, and the Giants led 3-0. They carried the lead into the next quarter.

Players on both teams were slipping and sliding everywhere. Backs trying to cut would have their feet fly from under them, receivers couldn't make the shape cuts on pass patterns and defenders would often slide right past the runners. It was miserable – and just right for the Monsters of the Midway.

In the second quarter the Giants, after three plays that didn't produce a first down, punted to the Bears. Because it was so slippery, the Bears' punt returner let the ball bounce, and the Bears started on their own 46. Nagurski went to work. Nothing fancy, just right up the gut, three, five, seven yards at a time. Finally, from the Giants' one-yard line, Nagurski carried three Giants into the end zone, and Jack Manders's kick made it 7-3.

The next time the Bears got the ball it was more of the same. Finally, the Giants stopped Nagurski and the Bears on their own nine. But Jack Manders nevertheless raised their score with a 24-yard field goal. On their next possession the Giants picked up a first down but were forced to punt. Again the Bears drove downfield, but this time Manders was wide to the right on a 38-yard attempt.

As the half ended the Giants were only down by a touchdown, but they knew they would need a miracle to beat this Bears team, especially on the frozen field. With that defense and with Nagurski, the Bears seemed to be in complete control. The score would have been even worse if two other touchdowns the Bears had apparently scored had not been called back because of penalties.

When the teams came out for the second half, everyone was startled to see the Giants in sneakers. The fans began laughing, and even the Bears were grinning. And during the third quarter it seemed that the sneakers wouldn't help. The Bears again marched down the field, and Manders kicked a field goal.

The fourth quarter begins, and the Giants still have both the icy field and the Bears to overcome to get back into the game. But now the sneakers begin to make a difference. The Giants' Ed Danowski passes deep to Ike Frankiun, but the Bears' Carl Brumbaugh closes in to intercept. There is a brief fight for the ball, but Frankiun has better traction. Brumbaugh slips, and Frankiun pulls it free and steps into the end zone. Giants fans race from the field to engulf Frankiun. The extra point is good, and it is Bears-13, Giants-10.

The Giants, sensing the tide turn towards them, rush the Bears' punter, Keith Molesworth, and his punt travels only 25 yards to the Bears' 48. Now Ken Strong takes over. He gets seven yards on his first carry, and on the next, he breaks into the Bears' secondary, and as the Bears come up to tackle him, he cuts on his sneakered feet and flashes past the Bears for a 41-yard touchdown run. By now the Polo Grounds is in an uproar, with fans hugging each other. Forgotten is the cold and discomfort. The Giants lead 17-13.

The Bears try to battle back but are forced to punt. Now Danowski rolls around right end and, with great blocking, takes it to the Bears' eleven. Ken Strong bursts up the middle and scores. Giants-23, Bears-13. The extra point is missed, but now the Giants are in complete control. The Bears' greatest

strength, Bronco Nagurski, can't get traction, and the Giants defenders are swarming all over him. In desperation the Bears try a trick play (that is today called a fleaflicker). Quarterback Gene Ronzani passes to a Bear receiver, who laterals back to Ronzani, who throws a long pass downfield. But Ronzani's pass is picked off by John Molenda, and the Giants have the ball on the Bears' 22.

With the crowd screaming for more, Danowski obliges. He picks up 10 yards off tackle, and on the next play he goes around right end, cuts back and scores easily. Giants-30, Bears-13. And suddenly the New York Giants are the champions of the National Football League.

There were Giants' heroes aplenty: Ed Danowski, Ken Strong, Frankiun, Mel Hein, Molenda. But the real hero was a still-unknown sporting goods dealer whom the Giants' equipment man knew. When called by the Giants, he brought every pair of gym shoes he had in his inventory to the Polo Grounds. And while in their own locker room the Chicago Bears were discussing strategy for the second half, the New York Football Giants were frantically trying to find 36 individual pairs of basketball shoes that would fit. There was no talk about blocking or special plays. All they could think of was that Danowski needed a size 10, Hein a 14 and so on. In the end, not all the fits may have been great, but the idea certainly was.

The 'Sneaker Game' was talked about for weeks in New York and in the national media. This one game generated more publicity for pro football than anything since Grange's debut in Gotham nine years earlier. It was the stuff that legends are made of, and it came at a time when legends were just what pro football wanted.

ABOVE: *Even without traction Nagurski was a tough man to stop. In this play on the icy Polo Grounds turf he made eight yards.*

BELOW: *1967 Pro Hall of Famer Ken Strong played with the Giants for eight seasons. In 1944 he led the league in fieldgoals.*

Notre Dame beats Ohio State: 1935

While the Fighting Irish were the most famous team in college football in the 1920s and 1930s, a college in Columbus, Ohio, was quietly building a formidable reputation. By 1935 the Buckeyes of Ohio State University were every bit the powerhouse that Notre Dame was, perhaps even more so. On 2 November 1935 these two teams finally met for the first time. It was to prove to be one of the best college games ever played.

Notre Dame, like all of football, had suffered a tremendous loss when its great coach, Knute Rockne, died in a plane crash on the plains of Kansas in 1931. That he was the greatest college coach of all time is not in question. From 1918 through to 1930 his Notre Dame teams, playing the best opponents in the country, won 105 games, lost 12 and tied five, a winning percentage of almost 90. He was the most influential coach in the game, his clinics the best attended and his books the most widely read. Even more than his coaching, it was the way he handled his players, the lessons of life he taught them, that set Rockne apart. He wanted his players to have moral courage, initiative and common sense, and he selected them as much on the basis of their characters as on their physical abilities. He would have been successful at any career, for he was a born leader. He chose football, and the sport was much the greater for his being part of it.

The mantle of leadership of the Notre Dame football program had passed on to Elmer Layden by 1935, when the Irish travelled to Memorial Stadium on the campus of Ohio State University. Layden, one of the fabled Four Horsemen, had an excellent team coming into Columbus, but he was nevertheless the underdog against the powerful and unbeaten Buckeyes. Not even in his own great playing career had the Irish ever had to face a team as tough as this.

In the first half Ohio State completely dominated Notre Dame and led at halftime 13-0. The Buckeyes' line, led by Gomer Jones, a quick, strong guard who weighed 220 pounds, didn't allow the Irish anything whenever Notre Dame threatened their goal. Five times Notre Dame came into scoring range, and each time the Buckeyes rose to the occasion, stifling the Notre Dame running attack and stopping Andy Pilney, the Irish ace passer, cold. Like most Big Ten teams, the Buckeyes were ground-control-oriented, and the running backs of the Scarlet Scourge, as someone dubbed the Buckeyes, moved almost at will behind the blocking of that big line. Their great sophomore halfback, Joe Williams, had completely outshone even the famous and redoubtable Andy Pilney.

By the time the third quarter had ended most of the huge crowd felt that it was all over. Even the few thousand Notre Dame diehards who had come from South Bend agreed. Notre Dame looked so hopelessly beaten that most of their fans had given up and just wanted the quarter to end without any further Buckeye scoring.

But they play 60 minutes of football, not 45, as Elmer Layden reminded his players before they took to the field for the last quarter. Whatever else Layden

LEFT: *Following Rockne's death one of his former Four Horsemen, Elmer Layden, became Notre Dame's next great coach.*

BELOW: *Layden's first great challenge was the 1935 Notre Dame-Ohio State game. The Buckeye line at first smothered the Irish.*

said may not have ranked with Rockne's 'Win One For The Gipper' speech, but it certainly must have been effective.

Andy Pilney led the way. Suddenly Pilney began hitting his receivers, and the Irish began moving. And Pilney, operating as the tailback in the Notre Dame formation, also began finding daylight for his runs. Down the field came Notre Dame, driving like wildmen. Pilney scored on an off tackle slant, and it was suddenly Ohio State-13, Notre Dame-6. But then the Irish missed the extra point!

Trailing by seven, with less than six minutes to go, the Irish got the ball back on a punt. Again, Pilney led the way. The great halfback from the streets of Chicago seemed unstoppable. His passing was deadly, and his slashing, swirling running brought the Irish right down the field. Again Notre Dame scored, but when they again missed the extra point, even Notre Dame's staunchest fans knew that now it was all over.

But the Notre Dame players don't. With only a minute to go, they stop Ohio State and take over on their own 49. Pilney drops back to pass, and the Ohio State defenders are all over him. He can't get the pass away, so he breaks to his right, trying to find any receiver. Then, suddenly, he breaks loose and takes off downfield. Twisting, spinning, fighting for every yard, the great halfback leaves Ohio State players strewn all over the grass. By the time the Buckeyes finally knock him out of bounds on their 19, the Notre Dame fans have gone wild, slapping and hugging each other. But slowly the cheering stops. Andy Pilney is lying on the sidelines, not moving.

Notre Dame and Ohio State players huddle near the sidelines, looking on as the Notre Dame doctor tends Pilney. There are 40 seconds left in the game. The doctor signals for a stretcher, and as the gallant Pilney is carried off, the whole stadium stands and cheers the Notre Dame star.

Pilney's replacement is a young man named Bill Shakespeare. Because Pilney has been the heart of the Notre Dame offense during the season, Shakespeare has had very little playing time. Few of the Notre Dame fans even know who he is, and Ohio State has little idea of what he can do. They can see he's no Pilney, for he is slight of stature and light in weight. With only 40 seconds to go, an untested tailback and 19 yards to gain, Ohio State's one-point lead seems secure.

Shakespeare tries a pass, but he is way off the mark. Thirty seconds to go. Now the Ohio State fans are standing and cheering. One more pass play, maybe two, and it's all over. In a sense, they are correct. Shakespeare fades to pass and looks deep. Wayne Milner, the Irish's best receiver, is covered. Shakespeare scrambles, and the seconds tick away. Suddenly, he stops and fires the ball toward the end zone. Milner is free, is over the goal line and

ABOVE: *In the second half the Irish finally got moving behind the running and passing of Andy Pilney. Here, their second TD. But as before, they miss the punt.*

TOP RIGHT: *Ohio's Frank Antenucci intercepts an Irish pass in the first period. He will lateral to Frank Boucher (10) who will go 65 yards for Ohio's first TD.*

BOTTOM RIGHT: *Notre Dame's almost unknown Bill Shakespeare came off the bench with 40 seconds left in the game to throw the winning pass to Milner.*

makes the catch. Bedlam breaks out as the gun sounds. Notre Dame-18, Ohio State-13.

Little Bill Shakespeare is swamped by his teammates, as is Wayne Milner. The Notre Dame fans climb over the grandstand wall and carry Irish players off the field, while 81,000 Ohio State fans sit, numbly, looking out on the field as their scarlet and grey Buckeyes walk towards their locker room. The invincible Buckeyes have been beaten, their dreams of a national championship gone. As the delirious Notre Dame fans tear down the goal posts, the Buckeye fans know how the fans of Army, Michigan, Stanford, Wisconsin and all the others feel when Notre Dame shakes down the thunder from the skies. It is all in the best Knute Rockne tradition.

Baugh leads the Redskins to the NFL Title

When George Preston Marshall purchased an NFL franchise for Boston, he hoped that his football team would be received by the Boston fans as enthusiastically as they had the baseball Red Sox. But although his Redskins won the Eastern Conference title, the Boston fans treated Marshall's team something akin to distain. So much so that when the Redskins were to face the Green Bay Packers for the NFL title game in Boston, Marshall decided to play the game out of town on a neutral site. Marshall's decision was vindicated when over 8000 paid to see Green Bay win. On 17 December 1936, a few days after the loss to the Packers, George Preston Marshall moved his franchise to Washington, DC. He had taken a financial bath in Beantown, and he knew that he needed a star attraction if he were not to suffer the same fate in the nation's capital. He found his star in Texas.

In the 1930s most football, both college and pro, was still run-dominated. Down in the Southwest, however, they threw the ball. And the man who threw it best was a tall, rawboned passing wizard named Sam Adrian Baugh from TCU. It took all of Marshall's considerable salesmanship to convince Baugh to play pro football. Baugh was a shortstop of considerable talent, and he had been signed to a baseball contract by the St Louis Cardinals, but Marshall's charm and money, plus the fact that the Cardinals had a shortstop named Marty Marion in their farm system, changed Baugh's mind.

When Marshall called Baugh in Texas to make arrangements for his debut in Washington, he told Baugh to buy some cowboy boots and a ten gallon hat. 'What size do you wear?', askedSammy.'They're for you!'shouted Marshall. So when Baugh, teetering on high-heeled cowboy boots he had never worn in his life, got off the plane in DC, George Preston Marshall was there with the whole Washington press corps to introduce the man he hoped would lead his Redskins to the happy hunting grounds where money and titles flowed.

Sam Baugh is remembered as a passer, but in games like 1936's Sugar Bowl he also ran brilliantly.

ABOVE: *The Washington Redskins, as they looked before the 1937 NFL title game with the Chicago Bears. In the backfield, left to right, are Ernie Pinckert, Riley Smith, Cliff Battles and the star of the game, Slingin' Sammy Baugh.*

RIGHT: *During practice before a game with the NY Giants in 1937 Baugh gets off a typically spectacular leaping pass.*

Many experts thought that Baugh was too skinny to survive the brutal play of the professionals. How wrong they were. For the next 16 seasons, Slingin' Sammy Baugh would lead the Redskins to championships and fill Griffith Stadium with cheering fans. He was the first really great passer to come to pro football. Arnie Herber and Cecil Isbell of Green Bay were good, but there was no one in the league like Baugh. Playing tailback in the Redskins' single wing offense, Slingin' Sammy showed all of football what a devastating weapon the forward pass could be in the hands of a gifted passer. Soon kids no longer wanted to be a star running back like Red Grange; they wanted to be passers. The story of how Baugh grew up throwing a football through a swinging tire hanging in his back yard became as well known as any legend in sports.

Baugh was easily the most accurate passer the game had seen up till then. He could fire a bullet pass 50 yards and hit his receiver in mid-stride. He could feather a pass over almost any defender into the receiver's arms. One day after practice before a big game, a reporter from the visiting city entered the Redskins' locker room to interview one of the 'Skins. As the players stripped and walked to the showers, he noticed that certain players had great red welts on their stomachs. When he asked why, he was told, 'Those are the receivers who've been catching Sammy's passes.'

Baugh was much more than just a passer. He was a surprisingly good runner on those skinny pipe stems he called legs. He was also probably the best punter in football, one year averaging over 70 yards a punt. He was, in addition, an outstanding defensive back, and he still holds the record for most pass interceptions in a game – four. In his 1937 rookie season Baugh had led the Redskins to the Eastern Division title. Now in the championship game, Sammy Baugh would face the Monsters of the Midway, the most physical and intimidating team in football, the Chicago Bears.

The game was to be played in Chicago at Wrigley Field. The day came up bitter cold, with the temperature hovering around 15 degrees. The field was frozen and ideal for the heavier Bears, who had Bronco Nagurski and a new running star to complement the battering Bronco, Jack Manders. To a young man from the plains of Texas, 15-degree temperatures, a frozen field and bone-chilling winds whipping off Lake Michigan did not exactly constitute ideal conditions for play. They weren't ideal for the 15,000 fans, either, but the spectacular game they were about to witness made them forget their misery.

If the Bears thought the wind and cold would make Baugh conservative, the first play showed them they were in for a long afternoon. On the very first play from scrimmage Baugh faded back. The Bears' defense broke through his protection, and the lanky passer ran to his right and, without stopping, fired a perfect bullet pass for a 40-yard completion to Cliff Battles. The Bears stiffened and eventually forced Baugh to punt, but that pass was a portent of things to come. When the Bears punted back to Washington, Baugh really went to work.

Passes to Riley Smith and Ernie Pinckert picked up 32 yards, and then Baugh and Battles ran for 21 yards, the last seven by Battles, and the Redskins were on the board first, 6-0. Smith's extra point, the first of four he would kick, put the visitors in the lead.

But these were the Chicago Bears, playing in front of their fans and in their kind of weather. Back they came. Bernie Masterson, the Bears' quarterback could also throw, and he hooked up with Jack Manders for a 51-yard gain. With Nagurski and Manders carrying the ball, the Bears moved to the 'Skins' 11, where Manders burst off a tackle to score and tied the game.

On the Redskins' next possession, Baugh's passes take the 'Skins downfield, but then the Bears intercept a Baugh pass deep in their territory and stop the Washington team. The Bears again march downfield, and the big play is another Masterson-to-Manders pass for 38 yards and a touchdown. Manders's kick makes it Bears-14, Redskins-7.

Now the Bears get rough. They try to put Baugh out of the game. But the Texan is tough and endures their pounding. Yet in the end, the frozen turf does to Baugh what the Bears can't. In the second quarter, the Bears catch Baugh just as he gets off a pass, and when he falls he hurts his left leg and sits out the rest of the second quarter. Without Sammy Baugh the Redskins can't catch up, can't get past midfield. But though the Bears threaten twice, Manders misses two field goal attempts.

When the third period begins, Sammy Baugh limps into the Redskins' huddle. In the next seven minutes he will put on the greatest passing exhibition so far seen in championship play. It takes him just four plays to go 70 yards, the last play a pass to Wayne Millner, who scores. The Redskins have tied the game.

The Bears, behind the running of Nagurski, come storming back. The great fullback, along with Ray Nolting, lead the charge as the Bears power running takes them to the 'Skins' four and a first down. The Bears try throwing quick passes, but the first two are broken up. On the third down the

LEFT: *Bears' quarterback Bernie Masterson was also a fine passer. In the title game his 51-yarder set up the Bears' first TD.*

RIGHT: *The Bears' Jack Manders made all three of Chicago's conversion kicks but missed two important fieldgoal tries.*

Best Wishes George
Jack Manders.
Minnesota
Chi Bear
8
10

Skins stop Nagurski at the two. On the fourth down Masterson fakes a handoff to Nagurski, jumps up and flips a short pass to Ed Manske for the score. The Bears take the lead, with Manders' kick, 21-14.

Before the Chicago faithful can get comfortable Slingin' Sammy Baugh goes to work. The 'Skins return the Bears' kickoff to their 23. On the first play Baugh dances back and spots Millner running down the middle of the field. He fires, and Millner takes it in stride at the 50 and goes all the way, 77 yards. Tie score.

When the Bears are held at midfield, they are forced to punt. The 'Skins let it go into the end zone and take it at their 20. Now Baugh and his runners move downfield. With fourth and one on the Bears' 42, the 'Skins gamble and go for it. Don Irwin dives over the stacked defense, and Washington has its first down. Baugh passes to Irwin for seven. Next he passes to Ed Justice for 35 and a touchdown. Three touchdowns in the third period, and the Redskins are now leading 28-21.

In the fourth period the Redskins get down to the Bears' 15, only to lose the ball on a Millner fumble. The Bears start back. Masterson hits Dick Plasman with a pass, and though Plasman has clear sailing, he is caught from behind by Baugh, bad leg and all. The two tumble into the middle of the Redskins' bench. Plasman gets up and throws a punch at Baugh, and both benches erupt. The fight that ensues is almost as good as the game, but finally order is restored, and they get back to playing football.

Now the Bears, with time running out, drive for the tying score. Moving behind Nagurski's running and Masterson's passing, they get to the Redskins' seven. But time is almost out. From the seven Masterson rolls right to pass, but the Redskins' great tackle, Turk Edwards, breaks through the blockers and throws him for a seven-yard loss. His next pass is incomplete, and the Redskins are champions of the National Football League.

On a day fit for Eskimos, Baugh had completed 18 passes for 335 yards and three touchdowns. He had thrown long and short, sideline passes and screens, and had run and punted, leading his team to its first championship. The tall Texan had brought the passing game to full flower on that frozen field in the Windy City. Others would subsequently break his records, but none would ever diminish the lustre of Slingin' Sammy Baugh.

Baugh, carrying, just before being tackled by the Bears' Sam Francis. Baugh ran three times for 32 yards and passed for 335.

THE SEVEN BLOCKS OF GRANITE AND THE DREAM BACKFIELD

ABOVE: *The climax of the celebrated Pitt-Fordham rivalry was their 1937 game. Here All American Pitt quarterback Marshall Goldberg of the Panthers' 'Dream Backfield' struggles for a two-yard gain against Fordham's 'Seven Blocks of Granite.'*

Players such as Sammy Baugh and his great college rival, Davy O'Brien of TCU, may have taught football how formidable a weapon the forward pass could be, but most teams, college and pro alike, were slow to learn the lesson. In fact, most of the games played during the years of the Great Depression were rushing duels. And peculiarly tough, relentless duels they were.

In essence they were small wars. Strong young men lined up nose to nose and crashed into one another, as blockers met defenders and tacklers hit the runners. They played without face masks, and the popular formations, the Notre Dame box and the single wing, were power formations, designed to overrun a defensive position, much like an infantry charge. Mass and power were the key elements in football. It might seem dull today, but back then football was seen as a test of a man's virility, his courage, his backbone. You stuck your face into a milling swarm of legs and bodies, and if your nose was broken afterwards, you simply wiped away the blood and lined up to repulse another charge. It was brutal, fundamental, a matter of the survival of the fittest.

Of all the college football series played at this time, the one that reflected the warlike nature of Depression football was the famous rivalry between the Fordham Rams and the Pitt Panthers. For three years these two powerful teams met and fought one another to a scoreless tie. In college football in the 1930s Pitt was as close to being a dynasty of power as college football had seen since the days of Knute Rockne at Notre Dame. The fact that Fordham was never the powerhouse that Pitt was is precisely what made these games so great. Pitt was favored each time, had the better players and should have won on talent alone. Yet year after year the Rams somehow managed to stop the Panthers in their tracks.

Both teams were led by famous coaches. Jock Sutherland coached Pitt, and his teams ran from the single wing. The dour Sutherland so abhorred the pass that when one of his quarterbacks threw two complete passes in a row, Sutherland benched him, sure that the third would be intercepted. His approach was to pull as many linemen as possible to lead his runners around the end. And when his blockers had knocked down the first line of defense, they went on to take care of the secondary. It was simple, powerful and physically shattering to the defense. Pittsburgh was so awesome that they beat Notre Dame five out of six times in the 1930s, and Notre Dame finally dropped Pitt from its schedule.

Fordham's coach was light years away from Sutherland. He was James Crowley, 'Sleepy Jim', formerly of Notre Dame and the Four Horsemen. The relaxed Crowley had come to Fordham from a successful stint at Michigan State. (One can see that if a coach would leave Michigan State for Fordham, football in the 1930s was a lot different than it is today.) Crowley was famous for his sense of humor. Football legend has it that once during half time of a Notre Dame game, Rockne was furious because Crowley had missed some assignment. 'Crowley,' shouted Rockne, 'do you know anything dumber than a dumb Irishman?' 'No, sir,' replied Crowley, 'unless it's a dumb Swede.' That broke up the whole team, including Rockne, and Notre Dame went out and won easily. Later, in New York, Crowley became a popular after-dinner speaker, regaling the audiences with Notre Dame and Rockne stories.

ABOVE: *Fordham coach 'Sleepy Jim' Crowley and Rams' captain John Druze in 1937. The year before, the Rams had allowed only one TD during the season.*

LEFT: *Pitt's dour coach Jock Sutherland believed in a brutal running game.*

The teams had met in 1935 for the first of the scoreless ties. Pitt, considered to have the most powerful running game in college ball, came to the Polo Grounds to face a team that had a defense nicknamed 'The Seven Blocks of Granite.' Thus it was offense against defense, and as often as Pitt would move down the field towards a score, Fordham would rise up and stop them. Fordham knew that Pitt wouldn't pass, and it therefore bunched eight or nine men on the line of scrimmage. Pitt just kept coming and coming, throwing blockers and runners at the tough Ram defense, and the defense bent but never broke.

One of the Seven Blocks of Granite was a guard, not tall but squat and powerful, weighing about 180 pounds. He was not the Blocks' best athlete, but he was probably their most tenacious. His name was Vince Lombardi, and years later he remembered facing those powerful charges of the Pitt Panthers. When he got to the pros as a coach, first with the New York Giants and later with the Green Bay Packers, Lombardi put in a play called the power sweep that was based on Sutherland's single wing sweep.

Fordham could not match the Pitt running game with an offense of its own. On offense, the Blocks carried out their assignments in more or less routine fashion. But when they were on defense they hit and fought like a Marine battalion on Iwo Jima. Time after time, just when Pitt felt the tide swing their way, one or all of the Blocks would stop them cold near the Fordham goal. They were deadly at stringing out the runner, and when they had their shot at him they never missed the tackle.

What happened in 1935 happened again in 1936. The same brutal, punishing, scoreless game, from which the frustrated Panthers would return to Pittsburgh bruised and battered. Marshall Goldberg, the great Pitt runner, remembers his teammates having to help him get into his berth on the Pullman. And he had a lower!

In 1937 the Panthers came to New York as defending Rose Bowl champions. They had crushed the Washington Huskies in the January classic and had been planning all summer long how they would score against Fordham. The 1937 Pittsburgh team is ranked in the school's history as their greatest ever. The Pitt backfield was being called 'the Dream Backfield' by the press, and only the Seven Blocks of Granite now stood in their way to another national title and a return to the Rose Bowl.

One of the Rams' Blocks of Granite in 1936 was Vince Lombardi, the future great Green Bay Packers coach.

RIGHT: *Pitt halfback Harry Stebbins hurls himself at the Granite Wall. He will gain only two yards for his efforts.*

BELOW: *The Seven Blocks of Granite varied over time. Thus Lombardi is not in this 1937 shot. Druze is far left.*

Just before the game, when the Fordham team was gathered near their dugout at the Polo Grounds, Jack Dempsey approached to wish the team luck. He told them to glory in their role as underdogs and said that he believed that they could whip the Panthers this time. If the Rams got an extra emotional shot from the old champ's pep talk, they would need it.

They stopped Pitt's first drive down the field and then got close enough to the Pitt goal line to try a 23-yard field goal, which failed. For the rest of the period the game settled down to the familiar standoff. Late in the second period the Panthers, on a 35-yard punt return, were deep into Fordham territory. A completed pass that brought Sutherland to his feet and three runs by Marshall Goldberg had the Panthers on the Fordham five. Even Rams' loyalists sensed that this time the Panthers would score.

Sutherland had known that he had to come up with something new to get by that fierce defense of the Blocks. So he had designed a play called '318', halfback-to-halfback reverse. Harold Stebbins took the snap from the center, and as he headed left towards the hole, he slipped the ball to Goldberg. While the Seven Blocks of Granite pursued Stebbins, Goldberg easily slipped into the Fordham end zone. Two years of not scoring had finally ended, and the Pitt faithful whooped it up. But the noise suddenly died, and then it was the Fordham fans cheering, for out on the field the referee was taking the ball from Goldberg and marching upfield, away from the Fordham goal. He placed the ball on the Rams' 20, turned to the crowd, put his left hand up in the air, grabbed his left wrist with his right hand and signaled, 'holding'. No Pitt touchdown. No glory for Marshall Goldberg. And the Seven Blocks of Granite still had not been scored on by the Pitt Panthers.

Although the teams had other chances to win the game, it seemed that the near touchdown and the hold-

ing call had somehow dispirited them both. Play became sloppy, with fumbling and other mistakes. It was as if they knew that they were not supposed to score, that this series was destined to be remembered for three scoreless ties. And so it is.

The next year Pitt finally beat Fordham 24-21, but by then the Dream Backfield and the Seven Blocks of Granite were gone, and it didn't mean as much. The game itself was changing. The T formation was on the horizon, and the brutal, man-to-man combat of the Fordham-Pitt games would become the stuff of 'remember when'.

Because they were the underdogs in each game, the fame of the Seven Blocks of Granite came close to matching that of the Four Horsemen, but in fact both teams were special. Whenever coaches and players talk about sheer toughness, giving and taking terrible punishment and never giving up, they'll always speak of Jock Sutherland and his powerful Panthers and Jim Crowley and his gallant Rams.

The Bears Crush The Redskins 1940

On a beautiful Sunday afternoon in Washington, DC, on 8 December 1940, the world of football changed forever. That afternoon the Chicago Bears utterly destroyed the Washington Redskins in the championship game. The 73-0 score was staggering, but it was the method by which the Bears accomplished their triumph that sent coaches in high schools, colleges and the NFL to their play books – not to study them, but to throw them out. The Chicago Bears had introduced football to the T formation.

The Bears did not invent the T. Actually, the T formation was the first formation that teams used back in the 1880s. Great early coaches such as Walter Camp, Amos Alonzo Stagg and Pop Warner had all used it. But the T fell out of favor because the coaches wanted more blocking for their runners and went to the single wing and the Notre Dame Box. George Halas, owner and coach of the Bears, continued to use the T all the years the Bears were playing, but it wasn't until a coaching genius named Clark Shaughnessy began visiting the Bears at their workouts (*ie* when his duties at the University of Chicago permitted him time) that the modern T formation began to take shape. Shaughnessy had plenty of time in the fall of 1939. The University of Chicago just couldn't compete with the other teams in the Big Ten, and when they hired the mercurial Robert M Hutchins as president, it hadn't taken him long to abolish football at Chicago.

With Halas, Shaughnessy began tinkering with the T, coming up with the man-in-motion and the countermoves. The great strength of the T was in giving the quarterback the opportunity to fake to one runner and hand the ball to another. The linemen didn't have to hold their blocks for long because the defenders usually were checked by the fake, and that allowed the ball carriers to slide through cracks in the defensive line. Speed, quickness and hard, slashing running were all keys to the T, but the fakes of the quarterback had to be believed by the defenders to make it work.

In 1940 Clark Shaughnessy moved west to Stanford University. In 1939 the Stanford football team had not won one college football game. Shaughnessy put in his T formation, coverting the tailback to quarterback and teaching Frankie Albert the spins and feints that a T quarterback had to master. He drilled Albert and the other backs on their fakes until players on the sidelines couldn't tell whom Albert had handed the ball to. The Stanford Indians finished the regular season undefeated and went on the beat Nebraska in the Rose Bowl.

During the regular 1940 season, the Redskins had defeated the Bears 7-3. They had stopped the Bears' running game cold and had defended against the Bears counter-plays perfectly. Halas called Shaughnessy and asked him to come back to Chicago to help the Bears prepare for Washington. Shaughnessy had time, since the football season at Stanford was over, and the Rose Bowl was a month away. So he came east and, with Halas and Sid Luckman, the Bears' quarterback, studied the films of the Bears' loss to the 'Skins.

LEFT: *A swarm of Bears, including Osmanski (9), McAfee (5), Fortman (21) and Siegel (6), descend on a hapless Redskin carrier in the 1940 massacre of the 'Skins.*

They threw out all the plays against which the 'Skins had successfully defended and concentrated on the plays that had succeeded. Then they added more counter-plays. But success still depended on their finding out if the Redskins would play the same defenses in the title game. So Shaughnessy put in three test plays that the Bears were to run the first time they had the ball. These plays would tell them what defenses the Redskins were using and would allow the Bears to use plays that would overcome those defenses.

It had been only three weeks since the Redskins had beaten the Bears, and George Preston Marshall had used the interval to taunt the Bears via the press. He called them crybabies and openly predicted that his team would win in a walk. What Marshall wanted was a big gate, and he got it. Marshall, ever the showman, had taken a leaf from the colleges and had put together a Redskin Marching Band, complete with Indian dress for the members and a magnificent headpiece for the drum major. He also commissioned a fight song, and 'Hail To The Redskins' duly took its place in the annals of American music. So, on this lovely winter Sunday, with band playing and crowd cheering, the Washington Redskins and the Chicago Bears took to the field.

The Bears had won the toss and elected to receive. On their first play from scrimmage, George McAfee cut off tackle for seven yards. The first play clearly showed that the 'Skins were playing the same defense they had three weeks before. Now Sid Luckman called the play that was to become one of the most famous in football history. McAfee went in motion to his right, and with the snap of the ball, the Bears' offensive linemen pulled to the right. The Redskins' linebackers began flowing to the right with McAfee, and Luckman took the snap and faked to Ray Nolting, as if he were running a sweep. Bill Osmanski, the fullback, had started off as if he were going to lead Nolting, but now he came back against the flow, and Luckman slipped him the ball. He headed outside the 'Skins' defensive tackle, but the line was bunched up there, so Osmanski bounced further outside, and in an instant the powerful, fast fullback was in the open and charging furiously down the sidelines.

Osmanski was almost in the clear, but two Washington secondary defenders seemed to have him pinned against the sidelines. Then George Wilson, the Bears' end, came across and blasted one 'Skins defender into the other, knocking both down, and Osmanski was on his way for 68 yards and the first score. After the extra point was made, the 'Skins took over, but the

ABOVE: *Clark Shaughnessy, the brilliant Stanford coach who instructed the Bears in the mysteries of the T formation.*

BELOW: *The mighty Bears of 1940: left to right (line) Wilson, Artoe, Musso, Turner, Fortman, Stydahar and Nowasky; (backfield) McAfee, Osmanski, Luckman and Nolting.*

ABOVE: *Bears quarterback Bill Osmanski is downed by the Redskins' Wee Willie Wilkin.*

RIGHT: *George McAfee, the Bears' halfback, carrying. Ten Bears scored 11 TDs in this game. McAfee's score came in the third period when he intercepted Roy Zimmerman's pass and ran 35 yards.*

Bears' defense quickly smothered them. Taking the punt from Sammy Baugh, the Bears went 80 yards, with Sid Luckman scoring on a quarterback sneak. The next time the Bears got the ball, Joe Maniaci went 42 yards to score, and it was Bears-21, Redskins-0 at the end of the first quarter. The Bears got seven more before halftime and went into the locker room ahead 28-0.

In the second half, it was even worse. Now the Bears' defenders got into the act, and the crowd began to wonder if they were going to outscore the Bears' offense. They intercepted five Redskins' passes, and George McAfee, Bulldog Turner and Hampton Pool all returned interceptions for touchdowns. Thus the defense got three touchdowns, but the Bears' offense still edged them by getting four. Halas sat Luckman down for the second half, and every Chicago player got into the game.

The Redskins' humiliation continued. The officials had to ask Halas to pass the ball late in the game for the extra point tries, since they were running out of new footballs. With the Bears ahead 73-0, the public address announcer somewhat tactlessly re-

ABOVE LEFT: *The year (1939) Bill Osmanski was drafted he led the NFL in rushing.*

ABOVE RIGHT: *George Halas didn't even bother to send his star quarterback, Sid Luckman, into the game in the second half.*

minded the crowd that 'season tickets for the Redskins' next season are on sale now.' The rest of his message was drowned in a hail of boos.

After the bloodbath was over and the 'Skins' survivors had escaped to the dressing room, the reporters were talking to Sammy Baugh. One asked, 'Sammy, do you think if Wayne Milner had caught your pass on the goal line early in the game, the score would have been different?'

'Sure,' replied Baugh. 'The score would have been 73-7.'

As word of the Bears' tremendous triumph spread around the country, Halas and Shaughnessy were besieged by coaches asking for any material they had that would explain the T formation. Films of the Redskins game were in such demand that Marshall began charging for them. In 1941, when Notre Dame hired Frank Lahey to become its head coach, he at once replaced the traditional Notre Dame shift and put in the T. Thanks to Shaughnessy and the Bears, the whole game of football was moving rapidly into the wide open game we see today. The great teams of the future would be led by quarterbacks who were passing wizards and clever tacticians. Men much like Sid Luckman.

NOTRE DAME v ARMY in the game of the century

On 7 December 1941 the Imperial Japanese Navy struck the United States forces at Pearl Harbor. Within a year, all the professional football teams were manned by rejects and old-timers whom the military wouldn't accept, and most of the college teams were similarly manned by seventeen-year-olds and 4Fs. The players were eager and willing, but the talent just wasn't there. There were, however, two exceptions to the rule: the service academies. Army and Navy, always strong, now dominated the college scene. Especially Army.

When Knute Rockne, Gus Dorais and the Notre Dame team travelled to West Point to play mighty Army in 1913, Army's greatest rival was Navy. But the loss to Notre Dame triggered a traditional rivalry that would soon displace that between Army and Navy. Army and Notre Dame played three more times before 1920, Army winning two and Notre Dame one. In 1928, the two teams met in Yankee Stadium, and again, the Irish defeated the favored Army team 12-6. But something happened before the game that forever changed the atmosphere of the Army-Notre Dame series. Notre Dame's first great All American had been a magnificent player named George Gipp. In the 1920 season George Gipp had been sick, but against Army he nevertheless led Notre Dame to such a brilliant victory that when he left the field the entire Corps of Cadets stood and applauded him. He died on 14 December 1920 of pneumonia.

After the 1928 victory in Yankee Stadium, a New York sports writer named Francis Wallace wrote that before the game Knute Rockne called his Notre Dame players together and spoke to them about George Gipp. 'On his

deathbed', he said, 'George Gipp told me that someday, when the time came, he wanted me to ask a Notre Dame team to beat Army for him.' And to complete the legend, when Jack Chevigny scored the winning touchdown for the Irish, he threw the ball into the air and shouted, 'That's one for the Gipper.'

When Wallace's sentimental story hit the newsstands the next day, the story of winning one for the Gipper made Notre Dame fans of every man, woman and child across the country. Unfortunately, it made the United States Military Academy the enemy whenever the two schools played football. The fans' bias was rewarded in the years that followed, for Notre Dame beat Army ten times and tied twice.

In 1943 Notre Dame was quarterbacked by Angelo Bertelli, who would win the Heisman trophy that year. But late in the season, before the Army game, Bertelli joined the Marine Corps. His replacement was an 18-year-old named Johnny Lujack. He led the Irish to a 26-0 victory, after which most of the rest of the Notre Dame team went off to war. By 1944 only Navy could give Army any competition. That year Army beat Notre Dame 59-0. In 1945, it was 48-0. But in 1946 the young men began to return from war, and college football began to get competitive again. Ever since Army had clobbered the Irish 59-0, all the nation had waited for the game when Notre Dame had its team back. For two years the press had written about this game, this battle to prove that Army was good only because the opposition was at war.

The Notre Dame team that came into Yankee Stadium in 1946 was undefeated. So was Army. Both had been ranked Number One in the country – Notre Dame in the AP pool and Army in the UPI pool. The coach of Notre Dame was Frank Leahy, and the coach of Army was Earl 'Red' Blaik. Both were great coaches, and both disliked each other. There were four All Amer-

ABOVE LEFT: *Notre Dame's legendary George Gipp. He was the best passer until Baugh.*

LEFT: *Army dominated college football in the first half of the 1940s. By 1945 its backfield of HB Bob Chabot, QB Y Arnold Tucker, FB Doc Blanchard and HB Glenn Davis was being called 'the greatest in history.' But it would be even better in 1946.*

ABOVE: *The 1945 Army-Notre Dame game was, as expected, a rout, Army winning 48-0. Here Notre Dame's Bill Gompers is being tackled by Army's great end George 'Barney' Poole in the third period.*

RIGHT: *Felix Anthony 'Doc' Blanchard, 'Mr Inside' of Army's daunting Blanchard-Davis combo.*

ABOVE: *The spectacular Army backfield of 1946: left to right, Tom 'Shorty' McWilliams, Young Arnold Tucker, Felix 'Doc' Blanchard and Glenn 'Junior' Davis.*

RIGHT: *Notre Dame's inspiring coach Frank Leahy had replaced the traditional Rockne Shift with the more modern T formation.*

icans at Notre Dame, and there were four on the Army team. Army's great strength was the running of Doc Blanchard and Glenn Davis, 'Mr Inside' and 'Mr Outside', both Heisman trophy winners. Their quarterback was a fine player named Young Arnold Tucker, and their veteran offensive line was led by Tex Coulter, another All American.

Notre Dame's star was the same Johnny Lujack who beat Army in 1943. He had returned from active duty aboad a submarine chaser. The Irish line was led by George Connors, a quick, fierce tackle, also an All American. In fact, Notre Dame had so much talent that All Americans sat on their bench. For most of the season, the team had not really been tested. But this was different. Now they were serious. Players took turns leading cheers in the huddle, something Leahy would never before have tolerated. When the scouts came in to talk to the team, they now found an intense audience, not the casual players they talked to before the other Notre Dame games. They were as pumped up and as emotionally high as Frank Leahy had ever seen a Notre Dame team.

At West Point the feelings were different, but just as intense. Army had to prove that they indeed were the better team, that they would beat a real Notre Dame team. They had gotten even with Notre Dame for all the defeats the Irish had inflicted on Army in the past years, but until they beat this Notre Dame team, with its galaxy of All Americans, the Army players knew their victories of 1944 and 1945 would be empty. During those years they had had to endure the taunts of the pro-Notre Dame civilians at Yankee Stadium, and now they vowed to silence the snide insinuations that they had played only weak teams while enjoying the comforts of West Point as the war was being fought.

So here came two teams, each with a mission to destroy the other. The hitting was tremendous. Both lines dominated play. Blanchard and Davis were continually stopped before they could get started. Lujack was constantly under pressure from the Army line. Once, in Notre Dame territory, Davis handed off to Blanchard on a reverse, and the big fullback got outside the Irish containment and sped down the sidelines toward a sure touchdown, only to have Lujack appear from nowhere, make a shoestring tackle and knock him out of bounds. And though Army then had a first down deep in Irish territory, Notre Dame pushed Army back out of scoring range.

Late in the third quarter, it was the Irish who drove deep toward the Army goal. With a fourth down on the Army four, Notre Dame shunned the field goal and ran for the first down. They didn't make it. Back and forth the teams went, with Army getting a little the better of it, but not enough ever to cross the Irish goal line. Davis and Blanchard, who had dominated college football with their running for two years, were constantly being unceremoniously dumped by the Irish linemen. Lujack was intercepted three times, and the Irish runners suffered the same fate as Blanchard and Davis.

The bitterness of the rivalry was never evident on the field. There were no injuries and only three penalties were called. When it was over, the players meet at midfield to shake hands and offer congratulations. They had played good, hard, clean football for 60 minutes, and when it was over, they were tied 0-0.

So ended the Game of the Century. Blanchard and Davis subsequently went into the military, Blanchard making it his career and retiring as a bird Colonel in the Air Force. Davis played some pro football after he got out of the service. Lujack went on to win the Heisman trophy and joined the Chicago Bears with the biggest contract in pro football so far. Frank Leahy's team would not lose a game until 1950 and would win three national championships.

The result of the great Army-Notre Dame contest of 1946 was a surprise, but looking back, it seems clear that it was the ideal outcome for such a match. It left both teams with honor and, at a stroke, wiped away a lot of old rancors. The dead past could bury its dead, and football could now look ahead to its bright new postwar future.

RIGHT: *Though injured, Notre Dame QB Johnny Lujack played the full game and prevented an Army score by tackling Blanchard singlehanded – a first.*

COLUMBIA UPSETS ARMY

ABOVE: *The scoreboard at New York's Baker Field records the upset of the decade.*

On 26 October 1947 the mighty Cadets of West Point came down the Hudson River to play feeble Columbia University at Baker Field. Since 1944 Army had not tasted defeat, and only the 0-0 tie with Notre Dame in 1945 and a 0-0 tie with Illinois in 1947 had kept its record from being perfect. In that period Army had scored 1292 points, while allowing its opposition just 192. They had shut out their opponents 18 times, and so far in 1947 not a single team had crossed their goal line.

Columbia was merely another weak opponent that Army had to brush aside before the real showdown next week with Notre Dame at South Bend. It would be the final game in the Notre Dame series, and since the scoreless tie of last year, both teams, and indeed the whole country, had eagerly been looking forward to the re-match.

Any thoughts that this edition of the Army football team would be markedly inferior to the last two had been dispelled in their first two games, as they routed Villanova and Colorado, holding both scoreless. The tie with Illinois had suggested that Coach Earl Blaik's team wasn't quite the powerhouse that had featured Glenn Davis and Doc Blanchard, but the new stars of the West Pointers, quarterback Arnold Galiffa and fullback Rip Rowan, were nearly as good, and in the first half of the Columbia game, the running of both almost made the fans forget the dynamic duo of 1946.

With the game less than five minutes old, Army went all the way to score the first time they had the ball. Rowan's running and Galiffa's passing took the Cadets 61 yards to the first score and quarterback Galiffa sneaked across the Lions' goal. Army also swept down the field the next time it had the ball, and only an interception in the end zone by Columbia stopped the drive.

Columbia had no running game to speak of, and its only offense was the pass. Even that was shaky, and Gene Rossides usually had to run for his life to escape being sacked by the huge Army linemen. So far, many of his passes had been off target, and only the amazing pass-catching ability of Bill Swiacki had given Columbia any completions.

In the second quarter Army drove down the field and scored when Rowan plunged the final yard. The extra point was good, and it was Army-14, Columbia-0. To no-one's surprise.

Columbia received Army's kickoff, and suddenly, Rossides began to find his receivers. He was still under great pressure from the Army line, since Army knew Columbia had no running attack, but with Swiacki making one sensational catch after another, Columbia began to make a contest of this mismatch. Three straight Rossides passes were caught and gained 53 yards, taking Columbia to Army's six. Rossides faked a pass and handed off to his halfback, Lou Kusserow, who split the Army defenders and scored.

The kick was good. For the first time this season Army had been scored upon.

On the next kickoff Army showed Columbia that it had no business being on the same field. Army marched down the field almost effortlessly, with Rip Rowan adding a splendid brokenfield run of 84 yards. As he crossed Columbia's goal, the Army team and their fans felt it was all over, and when the extra point was wide, little attention was paid. As the half ended, it was Army-20, Columbia-7. Thus the teams went into their lockers at halftime with Army in a commanding lead and having made a strong demonstration to Columbia that it could score almost at will. But the Lions of Columbia weren't buying that. The Rowan run had been brilliant, but the Lions still felt that their passing game could get them back into the ballgame. The big thing that Columbia had to do was to stop Army's offense.

They did just that. Much to the surprise of Army and to the delight of the Columbia rooters, the Lions held Army scoreless in the third period. They didn't score themselves, but stopping the more powerful Cadets boosted Columbia's spirits. And as the fourth period got underway, the Army players and coaches were feeling a little

ABOVE: *Columbia's Lou Kusserow being tackled by Army end Goble Bryant. Kusserow scored the Lions' first TD on a handoff after a fake.*

RIGHT: *Gene Rossides was Columbia's best passer, which was important, as the Lions had almost no running game.*

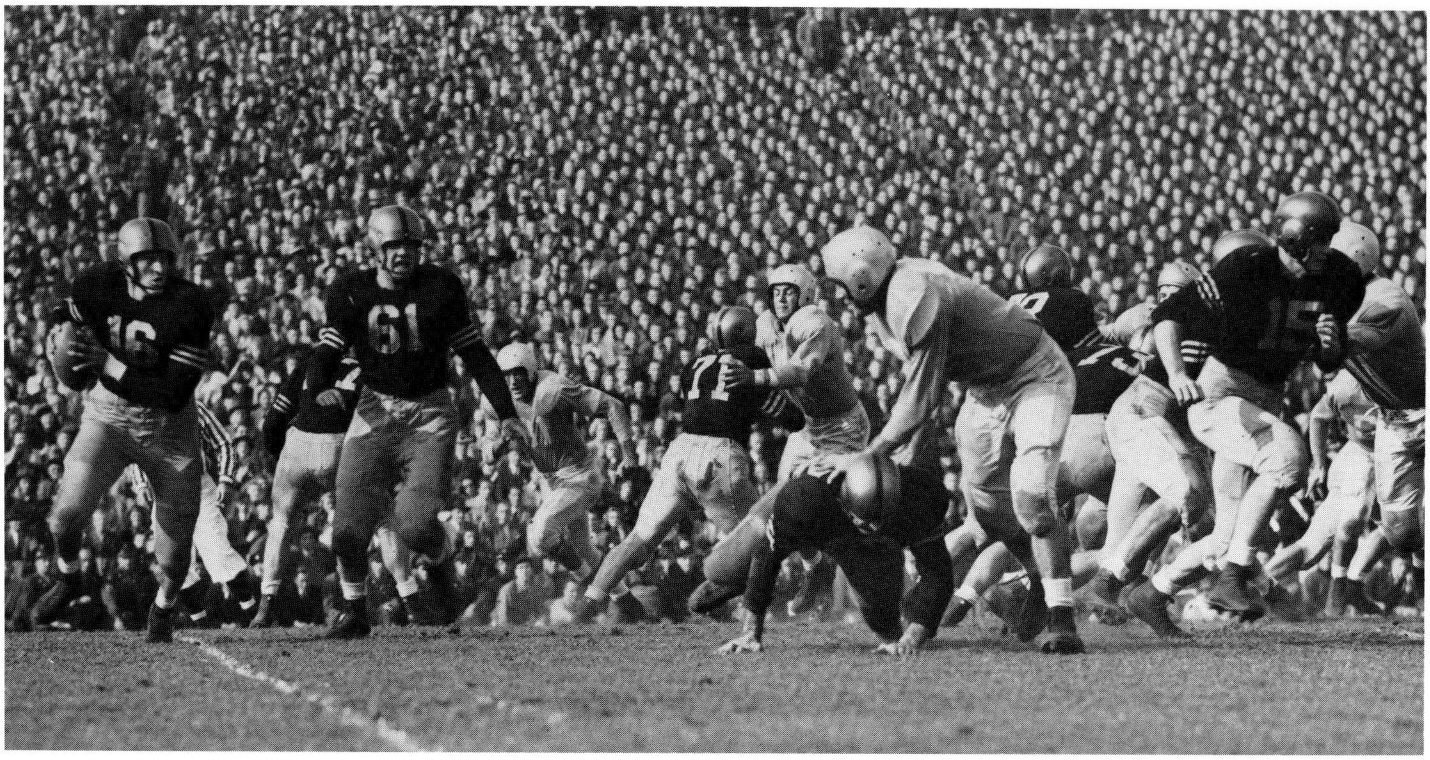

tense. The blowout they expected wasn't happening, and Columbia seemed to be getting stronger. Rossides had completed eight passes, and even if Swiacki's catches bordered on the unbelievable, they were still completions. Army was concerned.

Early in the last period, Rossides made two completions to Bill Olsen for 16 and 11 yards, and these, followed by a six-yard run, put the Lions deep in Army territory. Now Rossides faded back to pass, and the Army men swarmed in on him. He saw Swiacki cutting towards the corner of the end zone and threw. As the ball left his hands he was smashed to the ground by Army rushers and so didn't see Swiacki's catch. But seconds later, he heard a great roar from the stands. When Rossides climbed out from under the bodies of his Army pursuers, he saw the official with his hands raised signaling touchdown. Swiacki had dived for Rossides's pass and had skidded on one knee, catching the ball with his fingertips, before sliding across the out-of-bounds line just inside the end zone. With the extra point good, Columbia now only trailed Army by six.

Army stormed back. The kickoff was six yards deep into the Army end zone, but Bobby Jack Stuart ran it back 32 yards to the Army 27. From there Rowan ran for 18 and Stuart, seven. A Galiffa pass gave Army a first down on the Columbia 34. But now the Columbia defense came through again, stopping the Army attack cold and forcing a punt. When Columbia got the ball back on their 20, they had 80 yards to go to score.

ABOVE: *Many considered the Army QB, Arnold Galiffa, comparable to Blanchard and Davis. Here Galiffa (16), defended by captain-guard Joe Steffy, starts a run. He will be thrown for a nine-yard loss by Columbia end Bruce Gehrke.*

ABOVE RIGHT: *The Lion's Lou Kusserow holds the ball to his chest after being brought down by Army's Bill Gustafson. Kusserow made Columbia's winning TD.*

It took them all of one minute and 27 seconds and six plays. Rossides, now completely in charge of his game, masterfully directed the Lions. To stop Swiacki, Army was using a five-man line up front and dropping more men into the secondary. Rossides spotted this and handed off to Ventan Yablonski, who got to the Columbia 45. Next Rossides, faking a pass, got 22 yards on a quarterback draw. The fans at Baker Field were standing, screaming for Columbia. Army now moved into a six-man line. Rossides sent Swiacki deep, the great receiver cutting first towards the center of the field and then towards the sidelines. But even as Rossides threw he groaned inwardly. He had led Swiacki too much.

But Swiacki, who had amazed the multitude all afternoon with his circus catches, had one more for them. Somehow he dove for the ball, his body parallel to the ground, and just as Rossides's pass went by him, he seemed to stretch out to full length, catching the ball with his fingertips and holding on to it as his body slammed down on Army's three-yard line. Rossides gained a yard on the next play, and then Kusserow took it over for the

touchdown. With the crowd holding its breath, Yablonski calmly drilled the extra point through the uprights, and Columbia was ahead 21-20!

It was incredible. For the first time in years an Army team was trailing an opponent. But there were still six minutes left, and Army began another drive. Galiffa took to the air now, passing the Cadets up the field. But then, with two minutes to go, Kusserow stepped in front of one of his passes, and the great Army winning streak was history. The Columbia Lions – a team of little national prominence, an Ivy League team, a team that only a year earlier had lost to Army by 34 points, a team that was a four-touchdown underdog – became on this fall afternoon a team of legend.

BELOW: *The Lions' delirious celebration after the game. Aloft is Bill Swiacki. His fantastic catches of Rossides's passes was a key factor in Columbia's ability to break Army's 32-game winning streak.*

1950 THE BROWNS BEAT THE RAMS

When the All American Football Conference was formed in 1946, diehard National Football League fans ridiculed the upstart teams of the new league, calling them misfits and amateurs. The NFL itself openly laughed at the AAFC, saying that the worst NFL team could beat the champions of the new kids on the block. The AAFC lasted four years, and when the red ink and the empty seats in the stadiums forced the league to fold, the NFL magnanimously took over the three franchises that had made money, the Baltimore Colts, the San Francisco 49ers and the Cleveland Browns. The Browns had won every AAFC championship, but now the NFL fans were sure that the Browns would end up last in their league.

The Cleveland team had entered the AAFC as a charter member in 1946 with a head coach named Paul Brown. In 1945 Brown, formerly a coach at Ohio State, was coaching at the Great Lakes Naval Training Center. He had accumulated some outstanding college players who were then in the Navy, and the team was probably as good as some pro teams. Thus Brown's reputation as one of the best coaches in the country had in no way been dimmed by his work at Great Lakes. When newspaper man Arch Ward, organizer of the AAFC, offered a franchise to Mickey McBride, the owner of a taxi fleet in Cleveland, McBride asked Ward whom he should hire to run the team. The man Ward recommended was Paul Brown.

McBride contacted Brown at the Naval Station and made him an offer. Brown had planned to return to Ohio State, but the money McBride was offering was more than he could turn down. He had been making $9000 at Ohio State when he went into the service, and McBride now offered him $25,000, plus the general managership and a 15 percent ownership. Brown accepted and, while still at Great Lakes, began recruiting players for his new team.

ABOVE: *Lou Groza was the Cleveland Browns' great place-kicker/offensive tackle in 1950.*

LEFT: *Paul Brown, the coach who created the Browns in 1946.*

The players he signed were, to say the least, impressive. They would form the nucleus of teams that would win five straight championships and would quickly come to rival the dynasty that George Halas had created in Chicago with the Bears. Brown wasn't afraid to raid the teams in the NFL and took Edgar (Special Delivery) Jones from the Chicago Bears and Lou Rymkus, whom he had coached in Ohio State, from the Washington Redskins. When the Cleveland Rams announced that they were moving to Los Angeles, Brown immediately took several Rams players who didn't want to move west.

Some of the best college football players in the nation were still in the service when Brown began his stockpiling of talent. Many of them would not go back to school after the war ended but would nevertheless be eligible to play pro football because their classes had been graduated. From Ohio State Brown got three future Hall of Famers, Dante Lavelli, Bill Willis and Lou Groza. He had also seen a Utah pass receiver who had played against his Great Lakes team, one Mac Speedie, and he went after Speedie and signed him.

When Paul Brown had been coaching at Massillon High School the year before he took over at Ohio State, his team had been battered by the running of a fullback named Marion Motley. Brown had tried to get Motley to come to Ohio State, but Motley went instead to Nevada. Now Brown went

ABOVE: *One of many stars recruited by Brown was fullback Marion Motley.*

RIGHT: *Perhaps Brown's prize recruit was quarterback Otto Graham. In the 1950 Rams game Graham passed for 312 yards.*

after Motley and got him. Motley, in turn, told Brown about a teammate of his at Nevada who could kick a football further than any punter Motley had ever seen. So Paul Brown also signed Horace Gillom, who would become the best punter in pro football.

But perhaps the greatest prize of all was a tailback who had played against Brown's Ohio State teams. He was Otto Graham of Northwestern. Graham had been a fine triple-threat player for the Wildcats, and later, while stationed at North Carolina Pre-Flight, he had learned the intricacies of the T formation. Since Graham was an even better passer than runner, Brown thought he would be ideal as his quarterback.

So Paul Brown went into pro football in 1946 with the team he had personally built and was, appropriately, named for him. He would quickly become recognized as the most innovative coach in the game. He was the first coach to call all the plays for his quarterback, the first to make his players take intelligence tests, the first to grade his players and the first to make really extensive use of films of games. Brown ruled with an iron hand, would tolerate no interference in what he wanted and demanded professionalism from his players, both on and off the field. He would allow no drinking and insisted that his players wear jackets and ties on road trips and that they mind their table manners at dinner. If any player, no matter how talented, didn't obey Brown's rules, he was gone.

So now, in 1950, the Cleveland Browns, the team that had dominated the All American Football Conference, was about to be tested in the established NFL. Could they beat any NFL team? The Cleveland Browns would have a chance to answer that question in their first game in the NFL when they faced the Philadelphia Eagles. And in Philadelphia over 70,000 fans jammed the old municipal stadium to see their old pros teach these pushy newcomers a lesson.

The Eagles had won the NFL title in 1948 and 1949. They featured a powerful running game, led by the driving Steve Van Buren and a good passing game. But the strength of the Eagles was their defense. Many an offense had foundered on the rock-hard five-

BELOW: *Quarterback Bob Waterfield in 1945.*

man line of the Eagles. Earle 'Greasy' Neale, their coach, was from the old school that believed teams should physically man-handle the opposition. When the Eagles faced the Browns, their three interior defensive linemen weighed almost 280 pounds per man. For two years, these three big men, complimented by the defensive ends, had stymied every other team's running attack. And passing against the Eagles was almost as tough because of their fierce pass rush.

But the Eagles had not counted on the innovative coaching of Paul Brown. To neutralize the strength of the Eagles' defense, the three big men in the center, Brown had his offensive linemen gradually, almost imperceptibly, spread out during the first half. Since the Eagles' defenders lined up head-to-head with their offensive counterparts, this gradual spreading soon had the middle guard isolated. Now the Browns ran right at him, and the center blocked him in whatever direction the middle guard moved. Then the powerful Motley would shoot through the hole for huge gains.

When the Eagles came out in the second half, they had adjusted to try and stop the Browns' running attack. So now Graham's passing attack took over as he threw to Lavelli, Speedie or

his halfback, Dub Jones. The Eagles fans sat in awe as the Browns marched up and down the field against the supposedly impenetrable Eagles' defense. The shocking final score was Browns-35, Eagles-10.

The Browns had proven that they were worthy of the NFL, but were they worthy of the NFL's best? When the Browns were accepted into the NFL, they were put in the Eastern Conference, along with the New York Giants, the Pittsburgh Steelers, the Washington Redskins, the Chicago Cardinals and the Eagles. The team that had been the Cleveland Rams in 1945 had become the Los Angeles Rams in 1946. They played in the Western Conference, and in the late 1940s and early 1950s, the Rams had become the most exciting team in football. Their game was a passing game, with Bob Waterfield and Norm Van Brocklin doing most of the passing, and Elroy Hirsh and Tom Fears most of the catching. Fifty and even 70 points a game were nothing for Waterfield and Van Brocklin to put on the scoreboard. In 1950, the Rams had swept through the Western Conference winning their first six in a row and finishing the season in a flat-footed tie with the Chicago Bears, whom they beat 24-14 in a playoff. When the statisticians totaled up the Rams' showing for the 1950 season, they had set almost every offensive record in the books.

Most fans thought that the Browns win over the Eagles hadn't really proven anything, that the Eagles had taken them too lightly. Yet like the Rams in the West, the Browns ended up in a tie for the Eastern Conference title. And they finally won it – narrowly – with an 8-3 victory over the New York Giants. Now they would have a chance to show whether they had the stuff to make themselves champions of the whole league.

The weather that Sunday, Christmas Eve, in Cleveland was terrible. The temperature was below freezing and the winds off Lake Erie howled through the big park. It was so cold that only 28,000 diehards showed up to watch the championship game. What they and the audience of the first nationally televised NFL title game saw was one of pro football's greatest games. Both teams had super pass receivers, Hirsh and Fears for the Rams, and Speedie and Lavelli for the Browns. Marion Motley was the Browns' power fullback, and he was equally matched by the Rams' Bob Horner. The quarterbacks, Graham of Cleveland and Waterfield and Van Brocklin of the Rams, were the best in the game. They operated behind aggressive lines that blocked well for

LEFT: *Philadelphia Eagles star Steve Van Buren streams around end in the snowy 1948 playoff with the Cardinals.*

BELOW: *Because of injuries, Ram future Hall of Fame QB Norm Van Brocklin had to sit out the 1950 title game.*

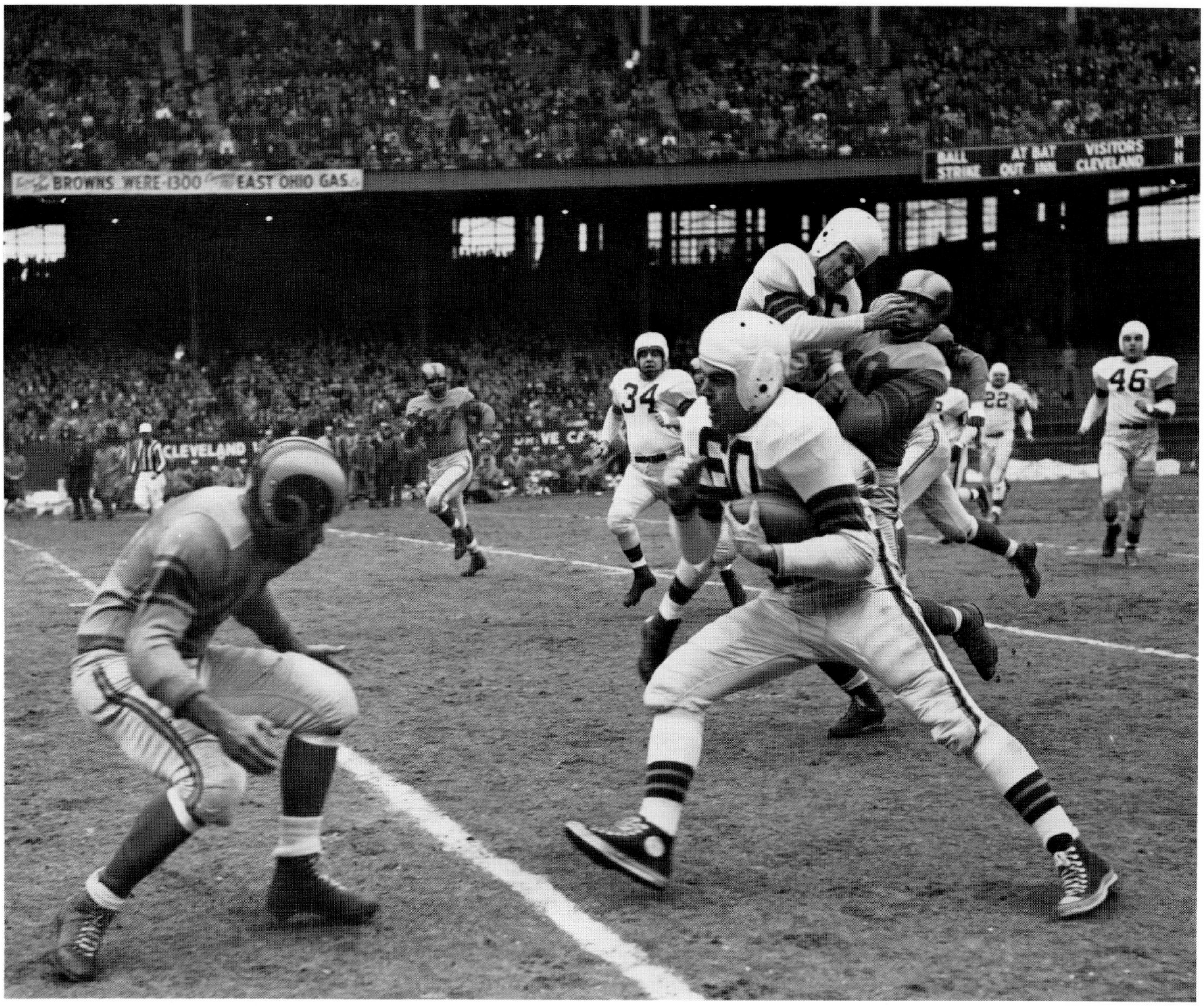

ABOVE: *Before the first quarter was half over three TDs had been made. Here Graham drives 12 yards in a series that would end in his 31-yard completion to Dub Jones and the first Browns score.*

both the pass and the run. In the kicking game, Bob Waterfield kicked the fieldgoals, as did Lou Groza for the Browns. The teams were well matched.

When the Los Angeles team came out on the field in Cleveland's Memorial Stadium, they were greeted by the hoots of the few brave fans huddled together, reminders that the fans hadn't forgotten the team that had left them four years earlier. The field was frozen and slippery. Glenn Davis, the famed Army halfback now playing for the Rams, had on shoes with special soles, but no other Rams player had them. The Browns came out wearing basketball sneakers.

The Browns kicked off, and the Rams could only get the ball back to their 18. Waterfield brought his team to the line of scrimmage, took the snap and dropped back. He spotted Davis on the 35, hit him, and Davis raced downfield and scored. With 27 gone, the Rams led 7-0 when Waterfield kicked the extra point. Waterfield's pass had been the longest touchdown pass in championship history.

Next in the first quarter the Browns' Graham, mixing his passes and Motleys' running, took the Browns downfield. His final pass of 31 yards to Dub Jones got the Browns six, and Groza's extra point tied the game. But in the same quarter, after a Gillom punt was downed in the end zone, Waterfield took the Rams 80 yards in eight plays, with Horner scoring from the three. Rams-14, Browns-7.

Back and forth they went. Graham's passing took the Browns the length of the field, a 35-yard completion to Dante Lavelli completing the drive with a touchdown. Groza lined up to kick the tying point, but the snap to Tommy James, his holder, was low. James tried to scramble, and he threw the ball to Tony Adamle in the end zone, but Adamle dropped it, and the Rams still led 14-13 at halftime.

On their first possession of the third quarter, the Browns march downfield, and again Graham hits Lavelli, this time for 39 yards and a score. The extra point makes it Browns-20, Rams-14. But the Rams respond, and quickly. They drive 71 yards on Waterfield's passing, and Horner scores from the one. Waterfield's kick gives the Rams back the lead, 21-20.

Now disaster strikes the Browns. The kickoff is fumbled, and when the Browns' runner comes out of the end zone, he only gets to the 12. On the very next play, Marion Motley fumbles the ball when hit, and the Rams' defensive end, Larry Brink, picks it up and runs seven yards into the end zone. In less than 25 seconds the Rams have scored 14 points and now lead 28-20.

The temperature is falling and snow is swirling around the field. As the final period starts the Browns need two scores to win. Graham starts them downfield with a completion to Speedie, and when his receivers are covered, Graham scrambles for another first down. Now the Browns are on the move. From the Rams' 14 Graham hits Rex Bumgardner for a touchdown, and with Groza's conversion, they again trail only by one.

All Cleveland needs now is to get within range of the Rams' goal, so that Groza can kick them into the lead. But now neither team seems able to move. At one point Graham manages to get to the Rams' 21 on a fake, but then he fumbles and the Rams recover. But the Rams can't capitalize and punt.

With one minute and 48 seconds left the Browns receive on their 32. On the first play Graham drops back to pass but can't find a receiver open. But Graham still knows how to run, and he takes off for a 14-yard gain before stepping out of bounds and stopping the clock. Graham next hits Bumgardner for 15, and he too steps out of bounds. Graham then spots Dub Jones for a first down on the Rams' 22. Now Graham fires a bullet pass to Bumgardner on the sidelines at the Rams' 11. He steps out of bounds and again stops the clock.

The Browns have one timeout left, and there are 40 seconds to go in the game. Graham brings the Browns to line of scrimmage and looks over the Rams' defense. Will he try another sidelines pass or a draw to Motley? Neither. Graham takes the snap and rolls to his right. He's tackled after a one-yard gain, but he doesn't care because he has the ball in the center of the field, ideally set up for Lou Groza.

It is only second down, but Graham trots off the field as Groza and the fieldgoal team come on. A hush falls over the huge oval. The teams line up, and Groza, head down, looks at the spot on the field where James's finger will be touching the ball. James looks at Groza and then at the center, Frank Gatski. He holds his arms out, fists closed. Then he opens his hands and Gatski snaps the ball back. It hits James right in the palms, and he quickly brings the ball down, turning so the laces will face forward. Groza has already begun his stride, head still down. His right foot slams into the ball. It soars into the air, over the leaping Rams, straight at the crossbar. And it is good! The final score is 30-28, and the Browns are the champions of pro football.

On a frozen field, playing against the magic of the great Rams' passing attack, the Cleveland Browns had brilliantly vindicated themselves, their coach and the reputation of their old league. They would go on to be the dominant team in pro football for the next five years, but their Christmas Eve victory against the Rams will always be remembered as their finest.

BELOW: *Browns coach Paul Brown and owner Mickey McBride flank Lou 'The Toe' Groza, whose fieldgoal won the game.*

Purdue upsets Notre Dame

When World War II ended, and the servicemen returned to their schools to get their degrees, the caliber of college football improved immediately. No longer were Army and Navy the sole major powers. A brilliant young coach had taken the reins at Oklahoma, and Bud Wilkinson was rapidly building the Sooners into a team to be feared. Herbert O 'Fritz' Crisler had led his Michigan Wolverines to resounding victories over the teams in the Big Ten. Lynn 'Pappy' Waldorf had gone out to California after coaching at Northwestern and had made the Golden Bears into one of the top teams in the country. There were quality teams everywhere, yet as before, the two that still dominated college football were the Black Knights of the Hudson, Army, and the Fighting Irish of Notre Dame.

From its first game of 1946 until its third game of 1950, Notre Dame won 37 games without a defeat, and only a 0-0 tie with Army in 1946 and a 14-14 tie with Southern California kept its record from being perfect. There were two main reasons for Notre Dame's dominance. First, though not necessarily foremost, Notre Dame, year in and year out, probably attracted the best football talent in the country. Kids dreamed about playing under the Golden Dome, and they came from all over the country to play in South Bend. Some were actively recruited, others were sent by alumni, but many just came of their own accord. The result was that these 1940s Notre Dame teams are today considered among the greatest ever to play college football.

But even with all that talent, someone had to mold and direct the players. And the Irish had a coach who, while not the charmer and extrovert that Knute Rockne had been, was every bit as good a coach. His name was Frank Leahy. He had played under Rockne at Notre Dame as a 150-pound tackle, and once when he was injured, he and Rockne had found themselves in adjoining beds at the Mayo Clinic, and the master had begun to talk to Leahy about the secrets of coaching.

Leahy served as assistant to Rockne before he was graduated. Then he went

BELOW: *A Notre Dame publicity shot taken early in 1950. The Irish had reason to be cocky, since they had been undefeated for four whole years.*

RIGHT: *In the 1949 Cotton Bowl SMU's Kyle Rote gave the Irish a big scare. He made all three SMU TDs and gained 261 yards.*

LEFT: *Not even Bob Williams, Notre Dame's fine quarterback could withstand the fiery 1950 Purdue Boilermakers.*

to Fordham to be the line coach for Sleepy Jim Crowley, whom he helped put together the Seven Blocks of Granite. From Fordham, Leahy went to Boston College, and in his two years there his teams won 20 and lost only two. In 1941 he returned to Notre Dame and took over the Irish.

Leahy had seen what the Chicago Bears had done to the Redskins, and he appreciated the high-powered scoring potential of their T formation. Until then, Notre Dame had run its plays from the Notre Dame box that Knute Rockne had created, but Leahy's first move was to jettison the Rockne shift and go to the T. The alumni thought that sacrilegious, and they let the new coach know it in thousands of protest letters. But when Leahy's teams started winning and winning, the alumni soon forgot the Rockne shift. And it didn't hurt that in Angelo Bertelli Leahy had the best college quarterback in the country at the time. In 1943 the Notre Dame team lost only one game to the almost professional Great Lakes Bluejackets, and that only in the last thirty seconds and without Bertelli in the lineup.

After the 1943 season, Leahy, like so many other college coaches, went to war, joining the Navy and seeing action in the South Pacific. He came back to South Bend in 1946, and between then and 1950 Notre Dame won the National Championship three times (Army winning the other). Because everyone treated Notre Dame as sort of the national college team, the Irish were expected to play teams in every section of the country. In 1949 that kind of scheduling almost caused the end of the Irish winning streak, when Notre Dame traveled to the Cotton Bowl in Dallas, Texas, to play Southern Methodist University.

The Irish came into Dallas a 27-point favorite. They barely escaped with their lives. The Mustangs were led that day by Kyle Rote, and he put on a show against the powerful Irish that is still the talk of college football. Rote scored the first SMU touchdown and throughout the afternoon, he ran and passed like a man inspired. Going into the fourth quarter the teams were tied 20-20. Late in the period the running of Emil Sitko and Billy Barrett took the Irish to SMU's six, where Barrett scored. Now it was 27-20, and only a few minutes were left. But SMU didn't quit. With Rote leading the way, SMU marched to the Irish 26. Then a tackle by huge Leon Hart knocked Rote out of the game. Fred Brenner, subbing for Rote, hit H R Russell, and the Mustangs were on the Irish five, with time running out. Rote came back in, but the big Irish defenders held him, and on fourth down, his pass into the end zone was intercepted as the gun went off. Notre Dame was undefeated again, for the fourth consecutive season, and although it had been given a terrific scare by SMU, the nation's press voted the Irish National Champions over Oklahoma, California and

10

LEFT: *Hero of the day for Purdue was QB Dale Samuels, whose brilliant passing set up all four of Purdue's touchdowns.*

ABOVE: *A Samuels pass, that Mike Maccioli ran 40 yards, produced the Purdue win.*

Army, which had also had perfect seasons.

Since his return from the war, Frank Leahy had had 36 victories, two ties and no defeats, a record that not even the great Knute Rockne could match. But as he headed into his fifth season, Leahy gloomily told the press that his team this year would not be as good as Notre Dame teams past. No one paid any attention. Leahy was well known for saying this kind of thing. In fact, before virtually any game he would insist that the upcoming opponent was clearly too tough for Notre Dame. After four years of such predictions, his statement about the 1950 team was duly ignored. After all, the Irish had an All American, Bob Williams, at quarterback, and even if many other All Americans from the 1949 team had been graduated, everyone knew that the Irish always had the horses.

In their 1950 opener, the Irish won over North Carolina 14-7. Not very impressive, but the fans and the press wrote it off, saying that the Irish were looking past the Tarheels to next week's game with Purdue, an old and honored rival. Although the two Indiana teams had been playing against each other for years, Notre Dame held a commanding lead in the series, the Boilermakers having won only four times since they began play back in 1896.

But this day would begin a new tradition. The crowd of 58,000 sat stunned as Purdue raced to a 21-0 lead in the first two quarters. Everything quarterback Dale Samuels and his Purdue teammates did worked, and nothing that Williams and the Irish tried worked. The Purdue lines beat the Notre Dame lines off the ball on both defense and offense, and Samuels's passing was brilliant. When Notre Dame trudged into the locker room at half time, the Notre Dame faithful could only pray that Frank Leahy would think of something to say that would inspire the Irish team.

And for a while it seemed that he had. The Irish recovered a fumble on the Purdue 10 at the beginning of the third period, and in one play they scored on a Williams pass. Purdue then drove back downfield, but a great goal-line stand stopped the Boilermakers on the one and kept the score 21-7. In their turn, Williams and the Irish marched back up the length of the field, and when Johnny Petitbon scored, the old stadium was in tumult. Purdue could feel that the momentum had passed to Notre Dame, and the Boilermakers knew that they had to do something. A seven-point lead wasn't enough against a team as good as Notre Dame.

Following the kickoff, Purdue moves to its own 44. Samuels tries two passes, but they fall incomplete. Notre Dame fans are yelling to the Irish to stop Purdue and force a punt, for there is still time for Notre Dame to score. But Samuels has risen to the occasion all day. Now he fades back. The Notre Dame rush breaks down the pass protection, but Samuels avoids the rushers, and as he leaves the pocket, he fires a pass to Mike Maccioli, his halfback, who has come out of the backfield and is open on the Irish 40. When he shakes off Petitbon's desperate diving tackle, he crosses the Irish goal, and Purdue wins 28-14. Over the next three decades, whenever Purdue played the Irish it would almost always enter the game as the underdog. And, as

ABOVE: *Neither Irish passing nor rushing was impressive in this game. They went on to their worst season since 1933: 4-4-1.*

RIGHT: *Notre Dame coach Francis William Leahy. His won-lost percentage was just shy of Rockne's – .888 v .897.*

in 1950, it would usually beat Notre Dame, and the player most responsible would be a young, unknown quarterback. The list of Purdue quarterbacks who have followed in the footsteps of Dale Samuels reads like a quarterbacks' Who's Who. Len Dawson, Bob Griese, Gary Danielson, and many more.

The Purdue team that won this victory had lost five straight games and was quarterbacked by a 161-pound sophomore from Chicago who had originally wanted to go to Notre Dame. But Frank Leahy had thought Dale Samuels too small for college football, so he went instead to Purdue. And today he had started something.

So the Notre Dame colossus finally tasted defeat. For four seasons, Notre Dame had dominated college football. They had played the very best everywhere in the country and had won and won. Their coach had proven to all that he deserved to be ranked with Rockne and the other greats of the past and present. In 1953, his team would go undefeated but be tied by Iowa and lose the National Championship to Maryland. Shortly thereafter, his health impaired from coaching, Frank Leahy retired from his post as head coach of the Irish. In his 11 seasons at Notre Dame, Leahy's teams won 87 games, lost only 11 and tied nine. He was a warm, intense, somewhat formal man, given to quoting poetry. He never swore and called his players 'Mister'. They loved him and won for him.

ARMY v NAVY 1950

The other great winning streak that a college team brought into the 1950 season was that of Army. Since their loss to Notre Dame in 1947 the Cadets had defeated all they had faced. For three seasons they had been undefeated, with only a tie by Navy in 1948 keeping them from perfection. On 2 December 1950 Army went to Philadelphia to play their ancient rival, the United States Naval Academy.

Among the 101,000 spectators were the Commander-in-Chief, President Harry S Truman, and Mrs Truman. Traditionally the Commander-in-Chief sat on the Army side for one half and the Navy side for the other half. But President Truman, acting on the advice of the Secret Service after his life had been threatened by Puerto Rican separatists, decided he would sit on the home field side throughout the game. Since the home field rotated each year, Mr Truman sat on the Navy

ABOVE: *The US Military Academy's Corps of Cadets in Philadelphia's Municipal Stadium before the 1950 Army-Navy game, one of the greatest upsets in this series.*

side, since the Middies were the home team this year.

Army was the 24-point favorite. Its 1950 team was being compared favorably to the juggernauts of the Blanchard-Davis era. Earl Blaik's team was blessed with two quality quarterbacks, his son, Bob, and Gil Reich. Army had a wealth of running backs, led by Al Pollard, Vic Pollock and Gil Stephenson. On the line was All American end Dan Foldberg, and many of the starters on the 1950 Army team had played in the big upset of Michigan the year earlier, when Army had broken Michigan's 25-game winning streak with a startling 21-7 victory.

The Navy team that Army expected to beat was made up of very young players who had won only a few games in 1950. In fact, Navy had not defeated Army since 1943. When team captains Foldberg of Army and Tom Bakke of Navy walked to President Truman's box for the coin toss and Navy won, many thought that the toss would be the only thing that Navy would win. And although Navy stopped Army three times deep in their territory in the first quarter, Navy seemed to be making no headway at all on offense.

Early in the second quarter, after Navy halfback Frank Hauff intercepted a Bob Blaik pass, Navy suddenly began to gain yardage against the heavier Army team. Fullback Dave Bannerman, Hauff and quarterback Bob Zastrow moved steadily downfield. From the Army seven, Zastrow faded to pass, then rolled to his right, eluded the Army tacklers and plunged into the end zone. White hats were flying everywhere, and when the extra point was good, incredibly, Navy had the lead, 7-0.

Army tried to come back, but now the Middies were playing like madmen. Every Army runner was brought down quickly by three, four or five Navy tacklers. The receivers were blanketed by the defensive backs, and Blaik, the quarterback, could never seem to find open receivers and had to run for his life.

As the second quarter wound down towards the half, Navy began another drive. A Zastrow pass to end Jim Baldinger for 30 yards finished the drive with a touchdown with only 20 seconds left in the half. Army was shellshocked. At no time during the season had any team played such a physical game with Army as had the smaller Middies. Earl Blaik now knew

RIGHT: *Navy's second TD was scored by Jim Baldinger (89) on a 31-yard pass from Bob Zastrow, the talented Navy quarterback.*

BELOW: *As Army captain Dan Foldberg and Navy captain Tom Bakke watch, President Harry S Truman tosses the coin to decide which team will make the first kickoff.*

that he and his team were in big trouble.

In the third quarter Army settled down, and their defense began to stop the runs of Navy and the passing of Zastrow. Navy's defense was still tough, but Bob Blaik's punting kept Navy deep in their territory throughout the quarter. Late in the quarter, Army flushed Zastrow out of the pocket and chased him into the end zone for a safety. When Navy's punt was short, Army was ready for business at midfield.

The fourth quarter is the wildest in the history of Army-Navy games. The Army defense is dominating the game now, thwarting all Navy offensive strikes. On the other hand, although Army's offense severely bends Navy's defense, it can't quite seem to break it. First Army batters its way down to Navy's 21, but John Gurski of Navy intercepts a Blaik pass to stop the drive. Navy promptly fumbles the ball back to Army on their 20, but again they stop Army in four downs and get the ball back on their 22. Army forces a punt and begins another drive into Navy territory. But Gerald Hart of Navy recovers a Martin fumble on their 29, and again Navy turns Army back. Time is now on Navy's side, but they still can't get a drive going and have to punt. The punt is blocked by Charlie Chirra and Elmer Stout, and Army has the ball deep in Navy territory yet again. But then another Blaik pass is picked off. When Army gets their last chance, they move the ball to the Navy three. With time running out, Blaik passes into the end zone to Foldberg, but John Gurski intercepts and takes off upfield. Time has run out, and as the Army tacklers finally stop Gurski at midfield, he fumbles and Army recovers. No matter. Navy wins 14-2!

All hell breaks loose as 3700 midshipmen climb down from the stands and carry the entire Navy football team around Memorial Stadium. The Corps of Cadets stands stunned in their places, unable to believe what they have seen. For the first time since most of them can remember a Navy football team has beaten Army. Seven classes of cadets and midshipmen had been graduated since this happened last.

RIGHT: *A four-photo sequence of Army's only score: 1. Zastrow (16) of Navy follows his interference as Army's Bob Volonnino (61) and Bill Rowecamp (82) rush in. 2. Zastrow tries to get off a pass, but Volonnino and Rowecamp are too close. 3. As other Army men – Kimmel (71) and Hart (68) – converge on the scene, Volonnino and Rowecamp push Zastrow back over his own goal line. 4. Zastrow is down, giving Army a two-point safety.*

To those who didn't know him, Earl Blaik seemed austere, distant and hard, yet his teams were utterly devoted to him. Coaching at West Point is unlike coaching any other school in the land except Navy. The cadets are up before dawn and in classes most of the day. Blaik only had them on the field for an hour and 15 minutes a day, and if a cadet player had a lab or a special test, he had to skip practice. Often Blaik had starters who regularly missed two practices a week. And there was no extra time when he could get his players together.

Because there were such demands on the cadets' time, Blaik had to be a superior organizer and teacher. Every practice was organized down to the nth degree, and many of the assistant coaches who learned at Blaik's knee went on to fine careers of their own. Vince Lombardi would later say that it was his training under Earl Blaik that turned things around for him.

Earl Blaik retired from West Point at the end of the 1958 season, a winning one. Since he left the academy, Army football has been in steady decline. People say that talented players today don't want to put up with the discipline of cadet life or miss the opportunity to play pro football. But they did it for Blaik, and they would do it again for someone with the dedication and intelligence and character of an Earl Blaik. But perhaps this greatest of Army coaches was one of a kind.

RIGHT: *Col Earl Henry 'Red' Blaik coached Army to its longest undefeated streaks: 32 games, 1944-7, and 28 games, 1947-50. He won three national championships and had three undefeated-untied seasons (1944-5 and 1949).*

ABOVE: *At the game's end, while the Cadets look gloomily on, ecstatic Navy fans set about demolishing goalposts.*

RIGHT: *Here Bob Blaik (15), one of Army's star quarterbacks and son of coach Earl Blaik, gains eight yards running after failing to find a receiver for his pass.*

The coach of the losing Army team was unaccustomed to defeat. Blaik had begun his coaching career in 1922 at the University of Wisconsin as an assistant to George Little. In 1927 he returned to his alma mater, West Point, to be an assistant to Biff Jones. In the 1930s he took over at Dartmouth and quickly made the Green Raiders an Eastern power, winning the Ivy League title twice. By the time he came back to the Academy to run their football program in 1942 only his arch rival, Frank Leahy of Notre Dame, had a better coaching record.

College football continued to draw the biggest crowds, but the pro game was catching on, enough so that television was becoming interested in it. The commissioner of the National Football League, Bert Bell, deeply distrusted this newest electronic marvel. Bell felt that no matter what the local television people would pay, it wouldn't make up for lost revenues from ticket sales. And it wouldn't help the NFL's image to have viewers see thousands of fans cleverly camouflaged as empty seats.

Bell wanted to control what games could be televised, so he devised a plan where the away games would be televised back to the home town of the visiting team, while the home games would be blacked out for a 75-mile area. Nevertheless the fans of the teams could now see their favorites when playing away, and the NFL soon began to get a good TV following. Moreover, the sale of tickets for home games began to climb.

As television brought more pro football to the viewers, new stars emerged. For example, the Chicago Cardinals were one of the worst teams in the NFL back then, but they had probably the best all-round player in the game. Big, blessed with great speed (he won a gold medal on the 1952 Olympic 400-meter relay team) and an uncanny ability to run in the broken field, Ollie Matson thus became one of the early pro stars that television brought to the nation. Other names the fans were getting to know were Hugh McElhenny, Joe Perry and Yelberton Abraham Tittle of the San Francisco 49ers, all future Hall of Famers. And another early star of the Western Conference was a brash free spirit named Bobby Layne of Detroit. The Lions had two Heisman trophy winners, Leon Hart of Notre Dame and Doak Walker of SMU, plus some other high-powered talent, but it was Bobby Layne who dominated the team. Layne couldn't pass as prettily as Graham, Waterfield or Van Brocklin, and he didn't look like a football player, for he had a slight pot belly and small shoulders, but when the game was on the line, Bobby Layne was one of the greatest 'money' quarterbacks of all time.

The Colts beat the Giants in overtime

In the Eastern Conference, dominated by the Cleveland Browns for five years, another team finally took over the spotlight in 1956. The New York Giants won the title and defeated the Chicago Bears in the championship game 47-7. What was important about this game was that the New York Giants had at last begun their return to being a power in the National Football League. And any time a team in New York starts to win and build a tradition, the media hype carries over into the coffers of the other teams. Television was beginning to capitalize on the popularity of the Giants in the New York area, and soon people were reading about Frank Gifford, Alex Webster, Charlie Conerly and other Giants heroes. But the most media attention was given to the Giants' defensive players. Often they would be introduced at the start of the game instead of the offensive players, as was the practice elsewhere in the league. Their special star was middle linebacker Sam Huff. When *Time* magazine did a cover story about Huff, the Giants' defenses and the middle linebackers in the league, publicizing defense became fashionable.

While in 1956 the Giants were winning the NFL title, a young quarterback was playing on the sandlots of western Pennsylvania for $6 a game. He had played college ball at Louisville and had even been drafted by the Pittsburgh Steelers, but he didn't make the final cut. When no other NFL team picked him up, Johnny Unitas played semi-pro ball and waited. A fan who saw Unitas play in one of those sandlot games wrote to the Colts about Unitas. General Manager Don Kellett read the letter and asked Unitas to come to Baltimore. He signed him almost immediately. Later, when asked why he signed Unitas, Kellett replied, 'Anytime you can sign a quarterback for nothing, sign him!'

LEFT: *Baltimore Colt QB Johnny Unitas. Already a star by 1958, his performance in the championship game with the NY Giants that year made him a hero.*

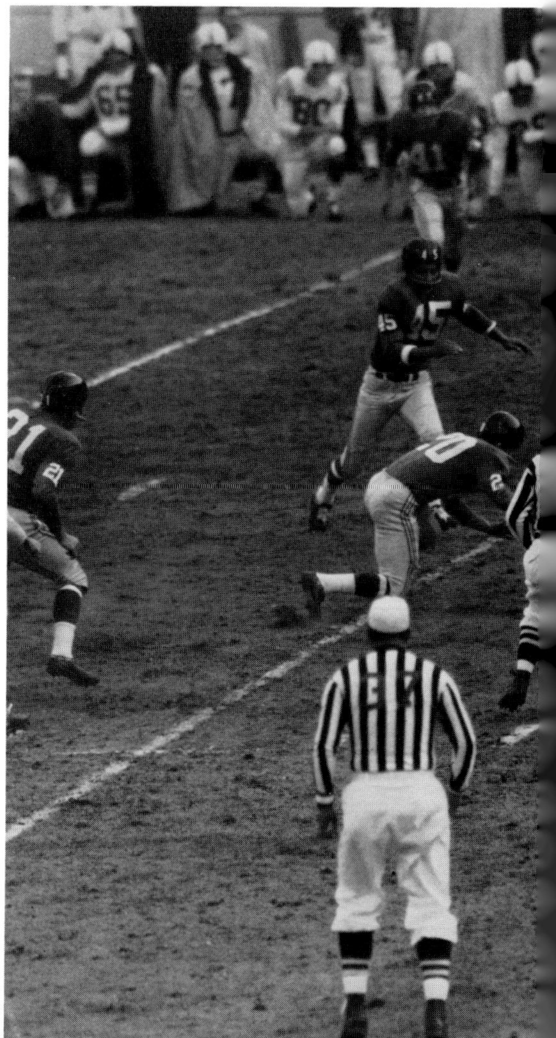

ABOVE: *Here, in 'the greatest pro football game ever played,' Alan 'The Horse' Ameche (35) scores the first Colts TD.*

LEFT: *Giants defensive back Jim Patton (20) dives for a fumble as Tunnell (45), Grier (76) and Modzelewski (77) assist.*

BELOW: *The Giants' backfield had in it such aces as QB Charlie Conerly.*

DRINK
Coca-Cola
TRIG
NATI ROADCASTING COMPAN

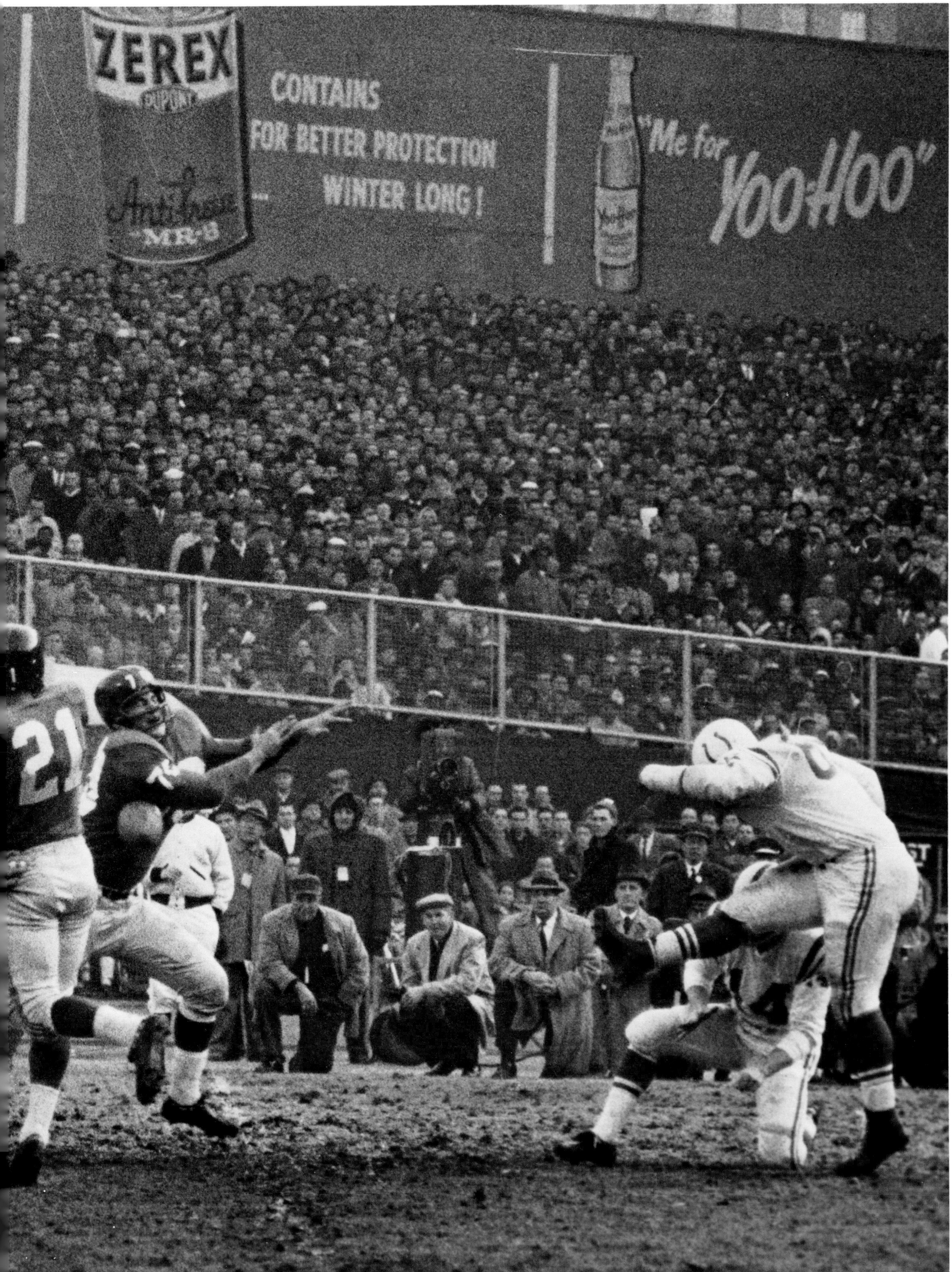
ZEREX
DUPONT
Anti-freeze
MR-8
CONTAINS
FOR BETTER PROTECTION
WINTER LONG!
"Me for YOO-HOO"

By the 1958 season John Unitas was already the most valuable player in the National Football League. Thus when the Colts and Giants won their respective conference titles and met in Yankee Stadium on 29 December 1958, the game would match the high-scoring Colts against the defensively powerful Giants. Obviously it was going to be a good game. What no one knew was that it was going to be possibly the most important game in the history of pro football.

PREVIOUS PAGE: *A first-quarter fieldgoal try by Steve Myhra is blocked by Giants Huff (70) and Karilivacz (21). Myhra's fourth-period fieldgoal would produce sudden death overtime.*

The fact that the Giants were representing the Eastern Conference was itself a story. They had beaten the Cleveland Browns three times during the season, twice in the regular schedule, tying the Browns in first place. In the second game, played in a swirling snowstorm at Yankee Stadium, the Giants won when Pat Summerall kicked a 47-yard field goal. When Summerall got to the sidelines after kicking the winning points, the offensive coordinator of the Giants came up to him and said, 'You know, you can't kick it that far.' 'I know,' replied Summerall to Vince Lombardi.

When the Giants ran out on the field of Yankee Stadium to meet the Colts, the 65,000 spectators who jammed the stands roared their affection and encouragement. But the experts still favored the Colts' chances because they had the better offense and because they had had an extra week of rest while the Giants and Browns had battled in the playoff game.

The experts seemed right on the button. In the first half it was all Colts. The Giants' offense seemed to have been left in the locker room, while the Baltimore defense, led by Gino Marchetti and Big Daddy Lipscomb, stopped Gifford and Webster and rushed Conerly so hard that his passing game was ineffective. Meanwhile, the Colts' offense was dazzling, with the passing of Unitas and the running of Alan Ameche and Lenny Moore.

The Giants did get the lead briefly in the first quarter, when Summerall kicked a fieldgoal, but the Colts then put two touchdowns on the scoreboard when Ameche scored on a short plunge and Unitas hit Raymond Berry for another six points. At halftime, the Colts went into the locker room leading by 11 points.

At the start of the third period the Colts charged down the field to a first down on the Giants' one. The Colts could put the game away with a touchdown, and the way they had been moving, it seemed that that was just what they were going to do. But the mighty Giants' defense now rose up and stopped them on the first three plays. With fourth and three, the Colts disdained the fieldgoal and went for six. Unitas tried a trap, but Cliff Livingston filled the gap and dropped fullback Alan Ameche on the five. The Giants' fans stood and roared.

As if inspired by the goal-line stand, the Giants' offense comes alive. From deep in their territory, it's Webster for six and Gifford for three and third down on their 14. Then Charlie Conerly fakes a run and throws a deep post pass to Kyle Rote. The former SMU great catches the ball near midfield and tears off downfield. The Colts' defenders catch Rote at their 25, and he fumbles when hit. But Alex Webster, who has trailed the play, picks Rote's fumble right off the ground and heads for the goal line. He gets knocked out of bounds at the one, but on the next play, Mel Triplett scores and it is now a ballgame, Colts-14, Giants-10.

Now, the Giants' defense is working to perfection, and nothing the great Unitas calls works. Sam Huff, Andy Robustelli, Jim Katcavage, Roosevelt Grier and Dick Modzelewski shut down the Colts' running game and

LEFT: *SMU's great Kyle Rote had been the Giants' bonus pick in the 1951 draft. He became one of their best receivers.*

pressure Unitas. The Giants' secondaries bat away passes and come up quick to stop the sweeps. This is Giants football. Early in the fourth quarter they take the lead. There are two big plays in this drive. Conerly hits Bob Schnelker for a 46-yard gain. Then Conerly passes to Frank Gifford, who makes a great catch along the sidelines and carries Milt Davis on his back into the end zone for six. Pat Summerall's extra point makes it Giants-17, Colts-14, with 10 minutes left. It is fitting that Gifford should have scored the go-ahead touchdown, for twice in the first quarter the great triple-threat halfback fumbled, and both times the Colts capitalized on his fumbles for touchdowns.

Now, with plenty of time left, Unitas and Colts start to come back. They drive to the Giants' 38 and go for a fieldgoal, something they should have done earlier when they had the ball on the Giants' three. When Bert Rechichar's fieldgoal kick falls short, the Colts rue that earlier no-fieldgoal decision even more.

Now the Colts defense gets tough, and when Phil King fumbles, the Colts have a golden opportunity. Unitas gets them to the Giants' 28, but Andy Robustelli and Jim Katcavage drop him for losses, and the Colts have to punt. When the Giants get the ball there are under three minutes left, and the darkness that has enveloped the stadium seems deeper on the Colts' side of the field. The Giants have a chance of running out the clock, but instead they try to run. On third down Gifford tries to cut upfield for the first down, but Gino Marchetti, the Colts' great defensive end, tackles him at the first down marker. When the players unpile, the ball is a few inches short of the first down and Marchetti is lying on the ground with a broken leg.

The huge Marchetti refuses to be taken to the locker room, so they wheel him off to the sidelines where he can watch the action. Now the Giants are inches from a first down, but it is fourth down, and they are deep in their own territory. If the Colts stop them on fourth down, they are close enough to kick a fieldgoal for the tie. With the Giants' fans screaming 'go for it,' Jim Lee Howell and Vince Lombardi confer and decide to punt. They have Don

ABOVE: *Colts' defender Gino Marchetti vainly tries to stop a Charley Conerly pass to Kyle Rote. But it was incomplete: this was not one of Rote's best games.*

Chandler, the best punter in football, and if he hits a good one, the Colts will be pinned deep in their territory with less than two minutes to go against their massive defense. It really is no decision. Everything calls for the punt.

Chandler's punt is a beauty, high and deep. When Unitas comes out on the field he has one minute and 58 seconds to go 86 yards against a defense that has stopped him all through the second half. Now Unitas calmly collects his team, and they begin their drive. They need to get a fieldgoal to tie and send the game into overtime. The Giants know this, but they are more afraid of the deep passing threat represented by Lenny Moore and set their defenses to stop the long bomb, a Unitas-Moore speciality. Unitas takes what the defense gives and combines with the brilliant Raymond Berry for three straight completions that move the ball into Giants territory. Berry's running helps get the ball to the

Giants' 13, and with seven seconds showing on the clock, the Colts take time out to set up for a Steve Myhra fieldgoal. With George Shaw holding, Myhra slices the kick from the 20, and it just barely curves through the goal posts. Score: Colts-17, Giants-17.

Overtime! For the first time in NFL history, a championship game goes into sudden death, and now these two great teams must play until one scores. The Giants win the toss and elect to receive. Two plays gain little, and when Charlie Conerly drops back to pass, he finds his receivers covered and tries to run for the first down. The Colts stop him short. When Don Chandler's punt is downed on the 20, the Colts have 80 yards to go.

Unitas coolly goes to work. His first call is a sweep to the right, and L G Dupre twists and turns to the 31. First down. Now Unitas gambles on a long pass to Lenny Moore deep down the sidelines, but Lindon Crow of the Giants, covering Moore one-on-one, tips it away. But Unitas hasn't wasted that pass. He has reminded the Giants' secondary that he'll go deep if he sees an opening. The Giants, having been burned by Berry in the fourth-quarter drive, try to help the defensive back covering Berry by having the linebacker drop back to assist him. Unitas reads this and completes a flare pass in the flat to Alan Ameche, and the Colts get another first down. The Giants stop the next two plays, and Unitas has third and fifteen. His next play is perhaps the most memorable in this memorable game.

Fading to pass, he rolls away from the strong Giants' rush. He looks for Lenny Moore, but he is covered. He then looks for his favorite receiver and spots Berry cutting towards the sidelines. But Berry isn't deep enough for a first down. So Unitas, with Giants racing towards him, coolly waves to Berry to go deeper. Berry does, and Unitas hits him with the first-down pass just as the Giants crash down on him.

After another sweep by Dupre that doesn't gain much, the wily Unitas takes advantage of the hard charge of Giants tackle Dick Modzelewski and calls for a draw to fullback Ameche. Art Spinney, the Colts' guard, traps Little Mo, tackle George Preas cuts off Sam Huff and 'The Horse' Ameche barrels through the hole for a 23-yard gain. Now the Colts are in fieldgoal range. A slant pass to Berry gets the ball to the Giants' nine yard line for first and 10.

The packed stadium is going crazy, exhorting the Giants to stop the Colts and at the same time cheering in admiration for the drive that Unitas and the Colts have executed. The field goal is ignored by Unitas, to the con-

ABOVE: *Baltimore's Alan Ameche is buried under a pile of Giants tacklers. At left is Jim Patton; right, Carl Karilivacz; on top, feet in the air, is Sam Huff.*

LEFT: *Three architects of the Colts' 23-17 victory. Left to right: Steve Myhra, John Unitas and Alan Ameche.*

sternation of the press box writers and other self-appointed experts. Unitas confuses them even further when he drops back and throws a down-and-out pass to his tight end, Jim Mutscheller, who catches it and is driven out on the one. Everyone knows what is coming next, and when Unitas hands off to Alan Ameche, the former Heisman winner from Wisconsin crashes into the Giants' end zone for the winning score: Baltimore Colts-23, New York Giants-17.

Thanks to Commissioner Bell's ruling, fans in the New York area were unable to watch this astonishing game on TV. (In fact, New Yorkers couldn't even read about it the next day, since the city was then in the midst of one of its periodic newspaper strikes). But plenty of other viewers could and did watch. It is estimated that the NBC live telecast of the game was received in nearly 11 million American homes, by far the biggest audience in football history. And, of course, within a few days everyone had heard about what Tex Maule of *Sports Illustrated* was calling 'The Best Football Game Ever Played.' The national popularity of televised football had been growing rapidly ever since the DuMont network had first broadcast the Rams-Browns 1950 championship game, but the Colts-Giants game was a TV breakthrough, a quantum leap not just into the bigtime, but into the supertime. The big networks began bidding against each other to televise pro games, and everywhere the sales of season tickets to the games of NFL teams soared. Within two years a group of investors and promoters eager to cash in on this bonanza had formed a rival league, the American Football League, and before long competition between the NFL and AFL for talent had begun to drive players' salaries to stratospheric levels.

Perhaps all this would have happened anyway. Perhaps the Colts-Giants game was just a fortuitous incident in an inevitable process. But there's no point in trying to second-guess history. The simple fact is that this single game utterly transformed the role that pro football played in American life. And the simple fact is also that it was one helluva game.

BELOW: *Colt Ray Berry also had a great game. His receiving in the fourth quarter helped set up Myhra's fieldgoal.*

THE PACKERS BEAT THE GIANTS: 1961

In the year when the American Football League was formed, 1959, an assistant coach of the New York Giants was busy packing his bags to move out to the NFL's equivalent of the Gulag Archipelago – Green Bay, Wisconsin. Vince Lombardi and his wife Marie got off the North Central Airlines flight from Chicago to Green Bay on a freezing February morning. His new job was to take over the reins of the oldest franchise in the league, a franchise that most owners wished would either fold or move to a bigger city. When the Packers came to play, fans stayed away by the thousands. Empty seats were not appreciated by the other owners, but getting the Packers out of Green Bay was almost impossible.

The Packers were the last small-town pro team left in America. They had been founded by a Notre Dame dropout named Earl 'Curly' Lambeau in 1919. Lambeau had persuaded the Indian Packing Company in Green Bay to back the team to the extent of buying them $500-worth of equipment. The team played in Hagemeister Brewery Park and supported itself – more or less – by passing the hat. (In the opening season each player made a grand total of $16.75). In 1922 Lambeau bought the team's franchise, retaining the team's

LEFT: *Halfback Johnny Blood (McNally) played for Green Bay 1929-33. In 15 seasons in pro ball he scored 224 points.*

name, Packers, simply because by then everyone in Green Bay was used to it. Green Bay loved the Packers, and with the hometown fans' support, Lambeau was gradually able to build a team capable of challenging the best. One of his earliest stars was another Notre Dame dropout, a brilliant running back named John McNally. McNally didn't think his name was sufficiently dramatic for pro ball, so, after seeing Rudolph Valentino in the film *Blood and Sand*, he promptly rechristened himself Johnny Blood. Blood, also known as 'the vagabond halfback,' led the Packers to three straight years (1929-31) in which they led the league in winning percentages.

The opening up of the passing rules

LEFT: *Vincent Thomas Lombardi, the Green Bay Packers' immortal coach, 1957-67. His record for those years: 89-29-4.*

ABOVE: *Hall of Famer Arnie Herber played for Green Bay 1930-40. In those years he passed for 6741 yards and 64 TDs.*

that George Preston Marshall and George Halas had forced on the NFL in 1933 benefited the Packers more than any pro team in the 1930s. In quarterback Arnie Herber, a hometown boy, they developed one of the NFL's best passers, and in 1935 Herber found his ideal receiver in a former college All Star named Don Hutson. In his debut against the Bears, Hutson caught a Herber pass on the first play and ran 83 yards for a touchdown, the first of 101 he would catch in his fabulous career with the Packers.

But those glorious days had been before World War II. Since the war the Packers had finished last or next to last virtually every season. Of their 1958 season, the season before the coming of Lombardi, Red Smith was able to write, 'The Packers have overwhelmed once (one win), underwhelmed eleven times (11 losses) and whelmed once (one tie).' Green Bay and the Packers still remained devoted to one another, but elsewhere in the league the Packers were hardly looked on as a great franchise.

In his first interview with the whole Packers' Board of Directors - there were 50 of them – Lombardi had made quite an impression. He had told them that he wanted to be both head coach as well as general manager. He had said that 'I have never been associated with a losing team, and I don't intend to be a loser in Green Bay.' He had insisted on absolute authority over everything in the Packers' organization, from the design of the uniform to the logo on their stationary. And he had said that if he didn't have complete control, he'd talk to the Eagles or wait for Jim Lee Howell to retire and take the much more glamorous job coaching the Giants in New York. The slightly stunned board had hired him and accepted every one of his conditions.

In the winter of 1959, as the snow covered Green Bay and the temperature hovered around zero, Vince Lombardi worked from dawn to late at night studying the game films of the Packers' 1958 season. He knew that he'd not get much help trading with the other teams in the NFL, since he was aware that the word around the league was that the only player on the Packers worth anything was their tackle, Forrest Gregg. Lombardi knew that for the most part he'd have to do with what he had on the Packers and what he got out of the draft.

He began to understand what a tremendous mountain he had to climb when he saw the situation at quarterback. He had a veteran, Vito 'Babe' Parilli, who had been a star at Kentucky but hadn't made it big in the pros. Backing him was a 17th-round draft choice named Bart Starr. The book on Starr was that he was too nice to be a pro quarterback and lacked both the arm and the leadership to be a winner. So Lombardi began looking over the rosters of the other teams to see if

ABOVE: *Bart Starr, the Packers' great QB, really hit his stride in 1961, when he passed for 2418 yards and 16 TDs.*

he could steal a professional quarterback. He couldn't, of course, get a star, but Lamar McHan, a backup with the Chicago Cardinals, was available, and Lombardi traded for him. He didn't cut Starr, but waited to see what he could do in training camp.

In reviewing the films, he noted that Paul Hornung, a Heisman Trophy winner from Notre Dame in 1957, had been used by the previous coaches as a quarterback. Hornung had been a quarterback with the Irish, but it seemed to Lombardi that he was more of a Split-T quarterback and didn't have the arm a pro quarterback must have. Yet Hornung was obviously one of the Packers' better runners. So Lombardi decided to try to mold Hornung into another Frank Gifford. He would make Hornung into a triple-threat halfback or kill them both in the attempt.

In his first meeting with the Packers' players that summer, Lombardi summed it up for them:

'Gentlemen, we are here to win football games. If we don't, you'll be gone, and so will I. I have no intention of leaving Green Bay.'

And then they went out to practice. Most of them thought they would die. He ran them until they dropped. He was everywhere, and the field echoed with his voice hollering. He introduced them to a Marquis de Sade evolution called the 'Nutcracker Drill', where a center, quarterback and running back lined up as they would in a game. To the right was a blocker. In front of his nose was a defender, with blocking dummies laying flat on either side of him. The drill was for the blocker to drive out the defender while the back ran through the hole between the dummies. Whenever the defender beat the blocker, there would be a major collision between the carrying back and the dummies. Everyone except quarterbacks had to participate, and Lombardi yelled the whole time. At the end of the first day, not one Packer player left his room after dinner. All were too tired.

But all the hard work and reassigning paid off. In their first league game the Packers played their arch-rivals, the Chicago Bears. When they beat the Bears 9-7, the Packers swept Lombardi onto their shoulders and carried him off the field. It would be a ritual that they would repeat often in the next nine years. With almost the same personnel who had lost 11 games in 1958, the Packers won seven games and lost five in Vince Lombardi's first season, practically the first winning season for the Green Bay Packers since the Ice Age.

In 1960 Lombardi and the Packers won the Western Conference title and played the Philadelphia Eagles for the NFL title. The Eagles beat them, 17-13. Afterwards, in a quiet, downcast Packers locker room, Lombardi called on the players to say a prayer of thanksgiving that nobody was seriously hurt. Then he said, 'I promise you that we will never lose a playoff game again.' And they never did.

Going into the 1961 season, the Packers were heavy favorites to win their conference title again. Their offense was now completely in the hands of

ABOVE: *Similar to Starr in 1961 was Giant Y A Tittle, who passed 2272 yards.*

LEFT: *One of several Hall of Famers in the '61 game: Packer Paul Hornung.*

Lombardi and his extension on the field, the new quarterback, Bart Starr. With Starr in the backfield were Jim Taylor, the rock-hard fullback, and Paul Hornung, who, in 1960, had set an NFL scoring record of 178 points in 12 games that stands to this day. The Packers won their in division and got ready to face the New York Giants.

In 1961 the Giants had pulled one of the great coups in the history of the game when, just before the season began, they traded a lineman to the San Francisco 49ers for passing great Y A Tittle. When Del Shofner of the Rams joined Tittle, the Giants suddenly had the best long-range passing attack in football, and although the Packers had narrowly defeated the Giants in a regular season game, when the Giants came to Green Bay for the championship game, they were favored.

One reason the Giants were favored was that the Packers' star halfback, linebacker and end were off on military duty, their National Guard units alerted because of a new Berlin Crisis.

ABOVE: *Yet another Packer great in this game was middle linebacker Ray Nitschke.*

Thus the Packers had to finish the season without Paul Hornung, while Ray Nitschke and Boyd Dowler could only get weekend passes to play in the last games. But late in the week before the title game, Pvt Paul Hornung walked into the Packers' locker room with a pass to play in the game. Vince Lombardi had campaigned for John F Kennedy in Wisconsin, both in the primaries and the election, and the White House had remembered the favor.

Lambeau Field was filled when the two teams met on 31 December. It was cold, but for winter in Green Bay, the field was in excellent shape. The Packers kicked off to the Giants, and Alex Webster returned the short kick to the 30. But the high-powered Giants offense didn't get a first down. The Packers' offense was hardly more successful, and so it went, back and forth, throughout most of the quarter. But just at the end of the quarter Starr got the Packers going. The big play was a swing pass to Hornung that the great halfback turned into a 27-yard gain, as he beautifully faked defensive back Jim Patton, the Giants' best open field tackler, and Sam Huff, their star linebacker. With runs by Taylor and Hornung, the quarter ended with the Packers on the Giants' five. On the first play of the second quarter, Hornung cut off tackle behind crisp blocking and barreled into the end zone. His extra point made it Packers-7, Giants-0.

Soon after the Packers' score, their aggressive 240-pound middle linebacker, Ray Nitschke picks off a Tittle pass and rumbles 23 yards deep into Giants territory. Two Starr passes are incomplete, but then he hits tight end Ron Kramer over the middle for 16 yards and a first down. Two runs by Taylor, and then Starr passes to Boyd Dowler for the touchdown. Hornung's extra point makes it Packers-14, Giants-0. Now the Giants must come back to stay in the game. Tittle knows this and goes to his favorite weapon, the deep pass to Del Shofner.

As he drops into his pass pocket, Tittle cocks and starts his arm forward, when suddenly Willie Davis blindsides him and only Tittle's strong hands prevent a fumble. He tries to screen a pass to take advantage of Davis's and the Packers' fierce pass rush, but the blocking breaks down, and he throws incomplete. The weak link in the Packers' pass defense had been reported to be defensive halfback Hank

RIGHT: *Paul Hornung (5) makes Green Bay's first score, dodging past Sam Huff (70) and Cliff Livingston (89) and pulling Dick Modzelewski (77) behind him.*

BELOW: *With the Packers leading 14-0 the Giants' Tittle (14) fades back for a long pass to Del Shofner but is blindsided by end Willie Davis (87). Tittle is flattened by Davis, and the pass is incomplete.*

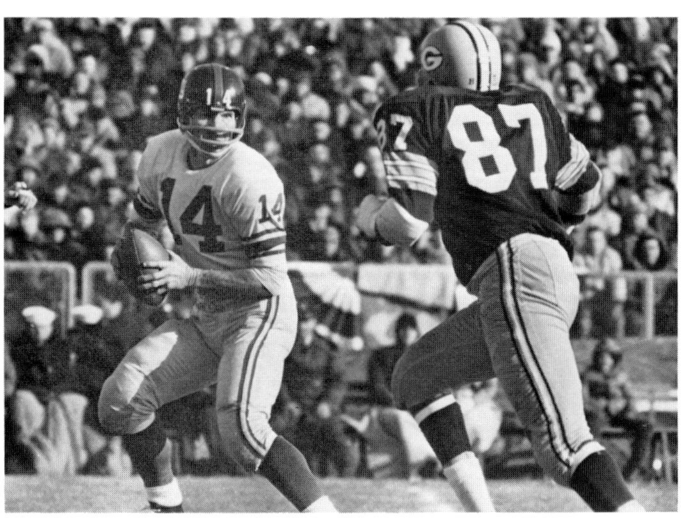

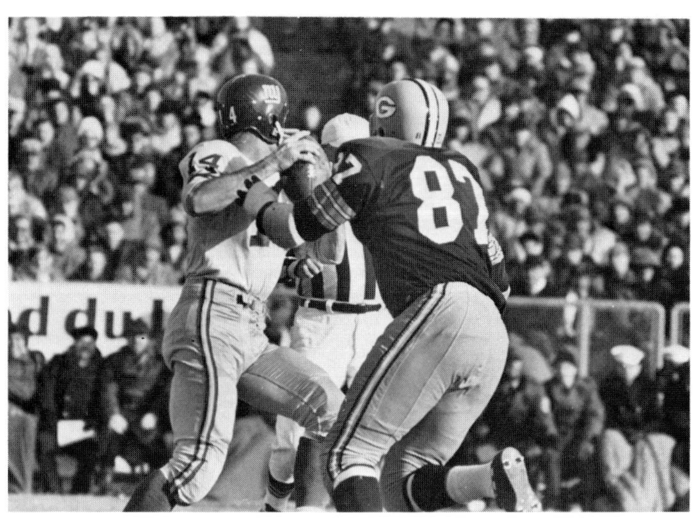

ABOVE: *Green Bay fullback Jim Taylor (31) plunges into the powerful Giants line for a gain of seven yards.*

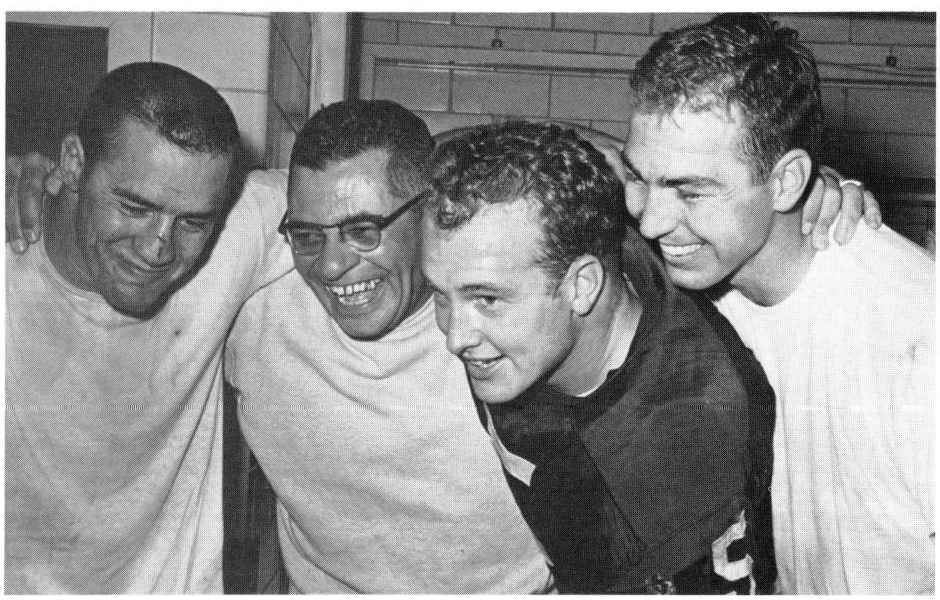

RIGHT: *In the Packers' dressing room after the game, left to right, Jim Taylor, Vince Lombardi, Paul Hornung and Bart Starr.*

Gremminger, so Tittle now sends Rote at Gremminger. But his plans are spoiled when Gremminger steps in front of Rote and intercepts on the Packers' 36.

Starr and the Packers know that this could be a decisive moment. If they can score now, the Giants will have to score more than three touchdowns against their defense. Starr sets to work, and Hornung and Taylor shred the Giants' line behind the superb blocking of Forrest Gregg, Ron Kramer, Jim Ringo, Fred Thurston and Bob Skoronski. Deep in Giants territory Starr calls a play that the Packers haven't even practiced that week. It is a flood pass. Both Hornung and Jim Taylor, with the snap of the ball, go out to the right side, drawing the free safety out to cover Hornung, while Sam Huff moves from his middle linebacker spot to cover Taylor. Tight end Ron Kramer blocks on the line of scrimmage, and when Huff goes out to cover Taylor, Kramer breaks over the middle. Starr hits him with the pass, and the big tight end runs over three Giants on his way to the touchdown. Thus the play that they hadn't practiced gets the Packers out in front 21-0. The half ends, as do the Giants' hopes.

In the third and fourth quarter, the Giants are hopelessly out of it. Green Bay moves up and down almost at will, and their defense completely stops Tittle. In the last quarter, desperately trying to escape a shutout, the Giants bring out 41-year-old Charlie Conerly. Conerly teams up with Kyle Rote and completes a 33-yard pass to get the Giants to the Packers' six. Then the Giants try the old halfback option pass that Lombardi put in when he was the Giants' offensive coordinator. With the Packers' fans cheering for a shutout, Bobby Gaiters, the Giants' halfback, takes the handoff from Conerly, swings to his right and throws to Rote in the end zone. But the pass misses by inches, and the Giants' last chance to score goes by the boards.

When the final gun sounds, the Packers pick up Vince Lombardi and carry him all the way to the locker room. Inside, the cheering and back slapping stops long enough for their habitual prayer of thanksgiving. Before they begin their celebration, Lombardi asks for quiet. He knows he only has a second to speak before he will begin to cry, so he tells them simply, 'On this day, you were the greatest team in the history of football.' His voice breaks, and he grabs Hornung and hugs him.

Without having practiced with the team or played in three weeks, Paul Hornung scored 19 points in that championship game, a record that still stands. Playing for the Packers in the game were nine men who would eventually be inducted into Pro Football's Hall of Fame: quarterback Bart Starr, halfback Paul Hornung, fullback Jim Taylor, tackle Forrest Gregg, center Jim Ringo, defensive backs Herb Adderley and Emlen Tunnell. The Giants would have defensive end Andy Robustelli, quarterback Y A Tittle, tackle Rosie Brown, middle linebacker Sam Huff and halfback Frank Gifford also going to the Hall.

Vince Lombardi is also in the Hall of Fame, and he coached them all.

The Thanksgiving Day Massacre

During the Lombardi years the Green Bay Packers had several intense rivalries with the top teams in the NFL. In the East, it was with the Giants, and in their own conference, with the Baltimore Colts, the Chicago Bears and the Detroit Lions. If there was one team that could beat Green Bay in the early 1960s, it was the Lions. The Detroit defense was one of the best in football, especially their front four and their middle linebacker, Joe Schmidt. To a man the Lions felt they were the better team in 1961 and should have been in the championship game. When Green Bay routed the Giants 37-0, Alex Karras, the Lions' great defensive tackle sneeringly said the Lions would have won by more. Going into the 1962 season the Lions were determined to prove their superiority over Green Bay.

They met at Lambeau Field in Green Bay in the third game of the season, both teams so far undefeated. In the first quarter the Packers managed to

ABOVE LEFT: *In an early 1962 game with the Packers Detroit QB Milt Plum called for a third-down pass that was intercepted.*

ABOVE RIGHT: *Among the Lions who swore they would never forgive Plum for his poor call was defensive tackle Alex Karras.*

drive deep enough into Lions territory for a Hornung fieldgoal, but for most of the rest of the half, the two defenses dominated the offenses. In the third quarter however, the Lions got a good field position on a Packers' mistake and scored. Then the Packers got another Hornung fieldgoal in the fourth quarter. But still the Lions led.

With nine minutes remaining, the Packers again drove deep into Lions territory. When Paul Hornung lined up for the go-ahead fieldgoal, there were still four minutes left in the game. But Hornung's kick fell well short of the goal posts, and now all the Lions had to do was to get a first down and run out the clock. The Lions got two first downs, and when the two minute warning was given they had a first down on their 46. Two plays got the Lions only two yards, and now, with less than two minutes to go, one of the most controversial calls in Lions history was made. Milt Plum, the Lions' quarterback, thought they needed another first down, so on third and eight, he called for a sideline pass pattern to Terry Barr. But Barr slipped on the wet field when making his cut, and Plum's pass went by his outstretched hands and into the stomach of Herb Adderley, the Packers' defensive back. Adderley took off down the sidelines, and the Lions only stopped him at their own 18. A few seconds later Hornung kicked the winning fieldgoal, and the Packers won 9-7.

The Lions were furious at Plum. They had had the league's leading punter on the sidelines, and all Plum had needed to do was call a simple running play and let their punter kick the Packers into a hole they couldn't get out of. When Alex Karras came into the Lions' locker room, he flung his helmet at Plum and had to be physically restrained from attacking his own quarterback.

After that close call, the Packers had a run of six more straight victories. *Time* magazine did a feature story on them, as did *Sports Illustrated*. The networks couldn't get enough of them, and week in and week out, one or more of the Packers was featured in some national magazine or television show. As Thanksgiving approached, and the Packers went to Detroit to play the Lions in the annual bash at Briggs (now Tigers) Stadium, they were still undefeated.

The traditional Thanksgiving Day football game had begun in the mid-1930s. Over the years the Lions had hosted most of the NFL teams, but since the early 1950s the Packers had always been the opponent. The Packers had beaten them in 1961 and this year went into the game a slight favorite. The Lions needed to win if they were to stay in contention in the Western Conference race, but that was a minor consideration to the Detroit players. They thirsted for revenge, and their rage at Milt Plum had subsided as Coach George Wilson managed to focus their anger on the Green Bay Packers. They hated Green Bay, especially Lombardi, whom they nicknamed 'the Jap' because of his toothy grin. Across the country, television sets were tuned into the local CBS station as millions waited to see the outcome of this well-publicized grudge match.

What they saw was raw fury, the ruthless destruction of one of the great teams in pro football history. The sellout crowd had barely settled in before it was on its feet, cheering. On his first pass in the game Bart Starr was thrown for a 15-yard loss by huge Roger Brown. This was only the beginning of the most humiliating day in Starr's great career. The Lions shut down the famed Lombardi sweep, stuffed Jimmy Taylor, the NFL's leading rusher and totally harassed Starr. Tackles Alex Karras and Roger Brown could do nothing wrong. Every time Joe Schmidt called a blitz, it worked. The Lions' defense was fantastic, and by the time the second quarter began, the whole nation was aware that the mighty Green Bay Packers could be this Thanksgiving's turkeys.

Milt Plum, still unforgiven by Karras, passed for two touchdowns in the second quarter. After receiving the kickoff, Starr knew the Packers had to score or the game was over. Trailing 14-0, he decided to go to his passing game. As he dropped back, Starr scanned downfield for his receivers, but suddenly, his vision was obscured by the gigantic form of Roger Brown flying at him. Brown smashed Starr to the ground, the ball flew free and Sam Williams, the Lions' defensive end, picked it up and rumbled into the end zone, as over 58,000 fans roared their approval.

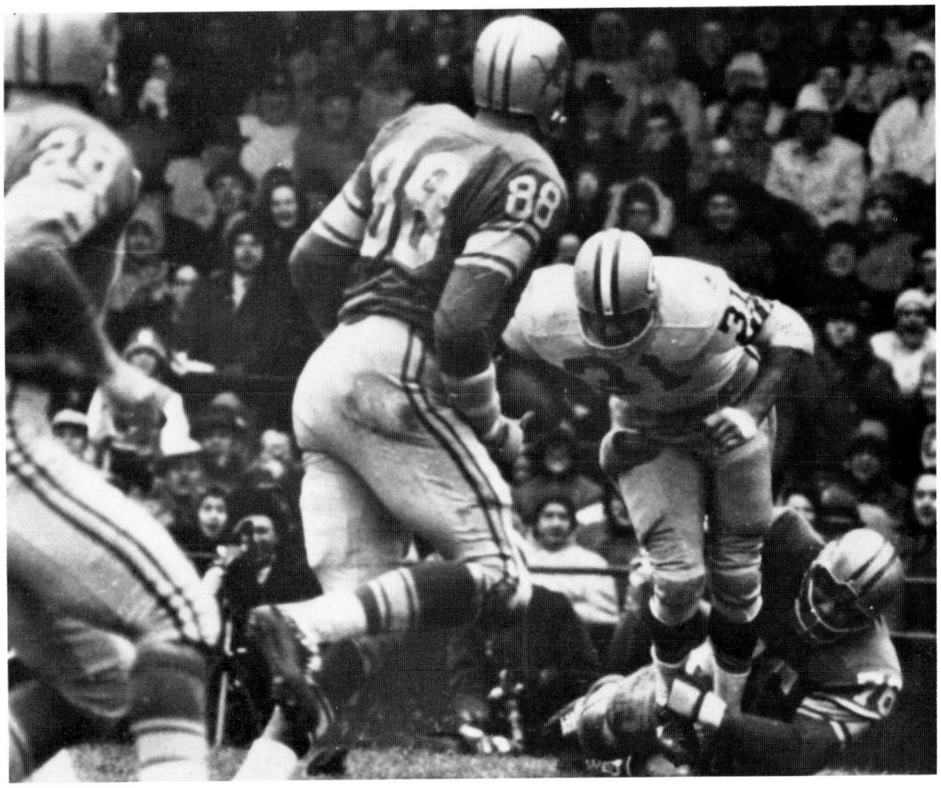

ABOVE LEFT: *Thanksgiving Day 1962: Detroit routs Green Bay. Here Lion Roger Brown traps Starr.*

ABOVE RIGHT: *Brown downs Jim Taylor.*

LEFT: *A typical scene from the Thanksgiving Day Massacre: Starr hopelessly beset by Lions Darris McCord, Karras and Brown.*

But there was more humiliation to be visited on the hated Packers. The Packers barely got out of their end zone when they received the next kickoff. When Starr dropped back into the end zone to pass, the entire Lions defense fell on him for a safety.

The Lions didn't maintain their explosive fury in the second half, and the Packers got a couple of touchdowns late in the game. But that meant nothing. The Detroit Lions had boasted that they were the better team, and on this Thanksgiving Day of 1962, they proved it to all of football. The final score, 26-14, may not look like a massacre, but that is nevertheless what it was. One statistic tells it all. In this game the Lions had thrown Bart Starr for no less than 110 yards in losses!

The Lions might have hoped that their example of how to beat Green Bay would lead other teams to emulate them and thus give them another crack at the Packers in the playoffs, but that didn't happen. Lombardi regrouped his troops, and they went the rest of the regular schedule undefeated. In December they beat the New York Giants 16-7 in the NFL title game, and thus finished the 1962 season with 12 wins and one defeat. But what a defeat!

SOUTHERN CAL v WISCONSIN
The Greatest Rose Bowl?

When, in 1902, the good people of Pasadena, California, decided that they needed something to hype their annual Festival of Roses, they had no idea what they were going to do to the football fans of America. The first game involved the University of Michigan against the Stanford Indians. Michigan was then considered to be one of the best in the country, but unlike today, teams from the West were seldom seen east of the Rockies. The Rose Bowl Committee decided to invite Michigan, since they wouldn't have as far to travel as Harvard or Yale, and that would keep expenses down. The fact that Michigan won 49-0 was duly noted, but no big deal was made of the game. But 14 years later, when the game was revived and began to be played on a regular basis, it soon did become a big deal, and has remained so ever since.

With the exception of Ohio State's playing in the Rose Bowl in 1921, the Big Ten had never come back to Pasadena at any time before World War II. But after the war the Rose Bowl Committee decided that the winner of the Pac Eight conference should represent the West each year in the Rose Bowl, and since they needed another conference to supply the opposition, they approached the Big Ten. The Big Ten had made it a practice not to play in Bowl games, feeling that football should end after the regular conference games were played. Winning the Big Ten title was honor enough, they felt.

BELOW: *The Rose Bowl. Many great games have been played here, but perhaps the 1963 USC-Wisconsin game was the best of all.*

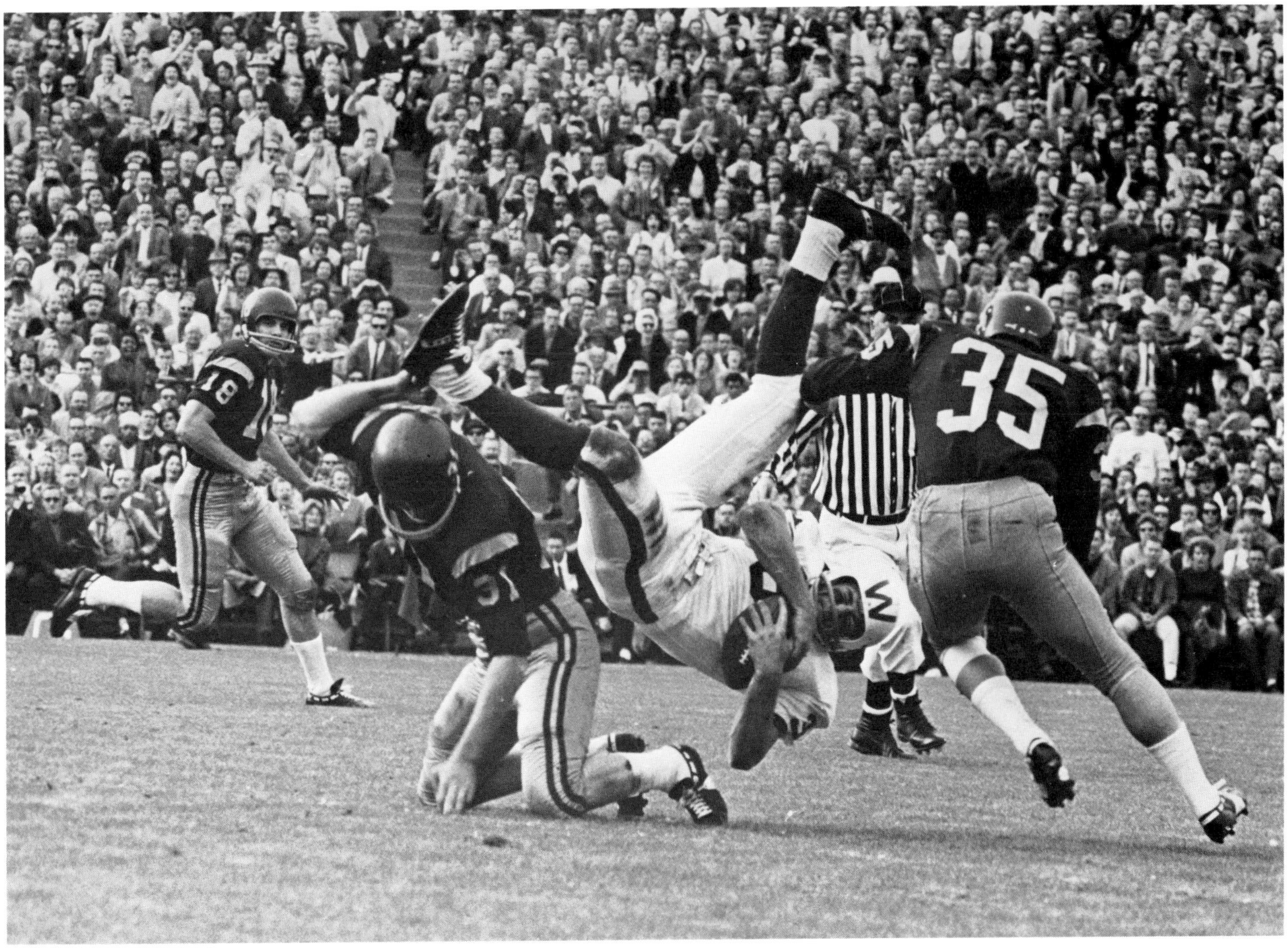

ABOVE: *The 1963 Rose Bowl game featured the two top-ranked teams in the nation and was doggedly fought by both of them.*

LEFT: *The four 'Bs' of USC: left to right, end Hal Bledsoe, quarterback Pete Beathard, linebacker Damon Baine and left halfback Willie Brown.*

But the Pac Eight made a great sales pitch, and the Big Ten signed on.

The first game between the two conferences under the new arrangement was to be played on New Year's Day 1947. But there was a problem. The Pac Eight representative was to be UCLA, and it had become apparent during the 1946 season that UCLA was in a class of college football with only Notre Dame or Army. UCLA was much too powerful for any Big Ten team that season, and it was tactfully suggested that the Big Ten wait until 1948 to play in the Rose Bowl. To make matters worse, the final winner of the Big Ten title was the University of Illinois, a not overly impressive team that had been beaten by Notre Dame. But Illinois said it was willing to face UCLA, so, with many misgivings, the Rose Bowl Committee went ahead and scheduled the game.

So UCLA, heavily favored to squash the Fighting Illini, went out on the field at the Coliseum and were promptly handed their heads. Illinois ran over, around and through the haughty Bruins, and when it was over, they had kicked UCLA all over Pasadena. The score was 47-14!

Between 1947 and 1962, the Pac Eight won only three times from the Big Ten. On New Year's Day 1963, the team representing the Pac Eight was the University of Southern California, undefeated and untied, ranked number one in the country. Their opposition was the University of Wisconsin, with eight wins and one loss and ranked number two in the nation. Thus, for the first time, two obviously well matched teams would meet in a Bowl game.

The teams were almost equally balanced in their passing and defensive games, but Southern Cal had an edge because their running game was a little

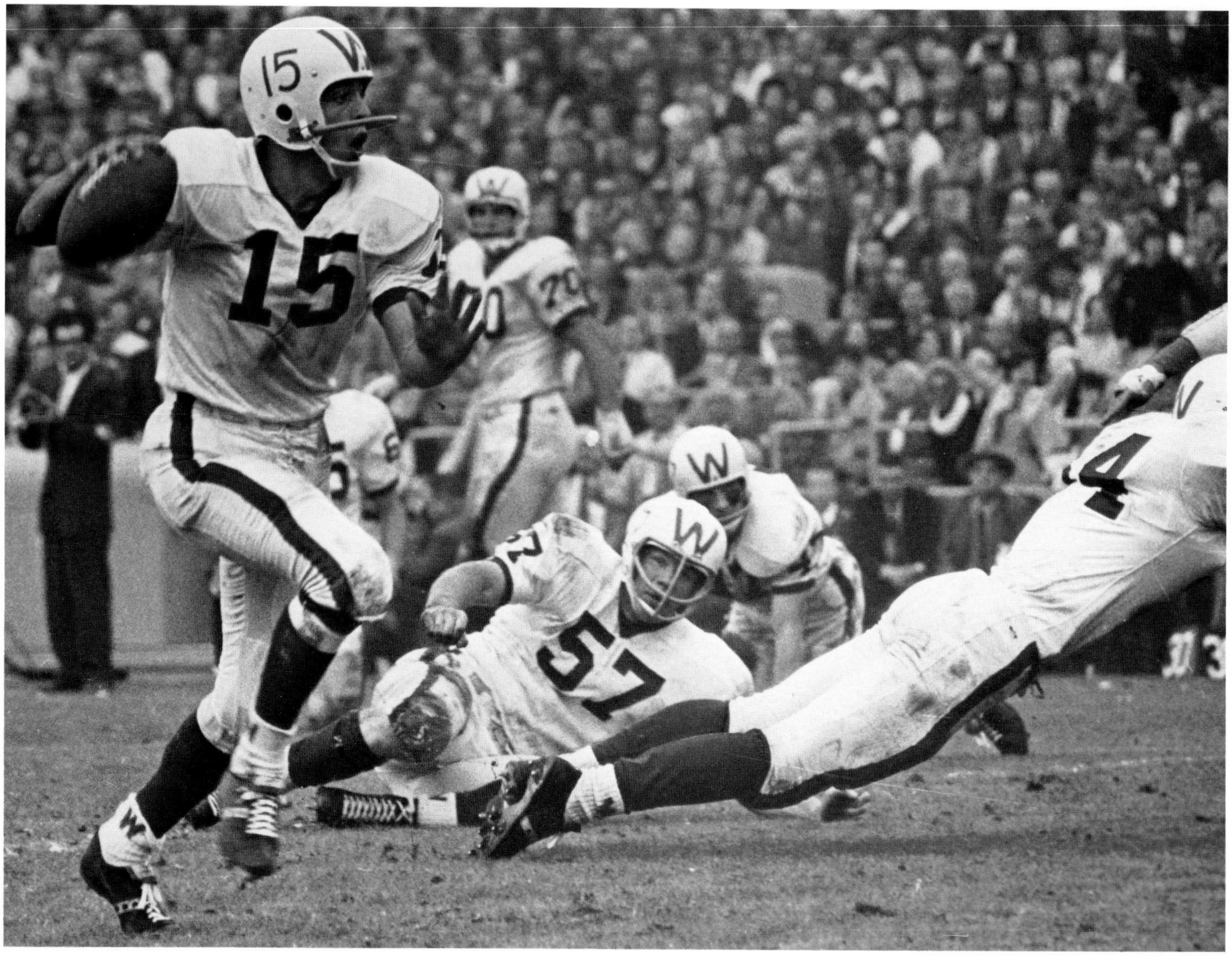

stronger. The first time Southern Cal got their hands on the ball they drove down near the Badgers' goal line. The tempo and style of the game was set on the next play. From the Wisconsin 13, Pete Beathard, the Trojans' quarterback, threw a touchdown pass to Ron Butcher, a tackle who had become an eligible pass receiver when they shifted just before the snap. It completely fooled the Badgers, and the Trojans jumped on top 7-0.

Wisconsin retaliated under the deft guidance of quarterback Ron VanderKelen, throwing to his All American end, Pat Richter. They tore back down the field, and their fullback scored from one yard out, tying the game.

In the second quarter it was all USC, as they put 14 more points on the board. VanderKelen had hit little Lou Holland for 30 yards and a touchdown, but the apparent score was disallowed by a holding call. So at the half, it was USC-21, Wisconsin-7.

It was almost 4 PM when the two teams came out to begin the third quarter. Wisconsin got back into the game with a touchdown early in the quarter, but Beathard, fullback Ben Wilson and halfback Willie Wilson kept the Trojans comfortably ahead by adding another 14 points.

As the sun begins to set over the Santa Ana Mountains, the lead of the Trojans seems insurmountable. But Ron VanderKelen and Pat Richter lead a furious Badgers comeback. VanderKelen is on fire. He has already stood the Trojans pass defense on its ear, and he brings the Badgers back with touchdown passes to Richter and halfback Gary Kroner. Suddenly, the Badgers are right back in the game, and the 98,000 fans are screaming for Wisconsin and their gutsy comeback.

Pete Beathard counters some of VanderKelen's heroics with a touchdown pass of his own to Fred Hill, and Willie Brown intercepts a VanderKelen pass in the end zone to snuff out Wisconsin's try to tie the game. Now the Wisconsin defense stiffens and holds the Trojans deep in their own territory. A poor snap to the Trojans' punter, Ernie Jones, sails into the end zone, and Jones wisely falls on the ball for a safety. There are less than five minutes left, and the score is Southern Cal-42, Wisconsin-30.

VanderKelen has broken all Rose Bowl passing records, and now he brings his Badgers relentlessly downfield. The Badgers score and there is still time, almost two minutes, when they kick off to the Trojans. But Wisconsin has spent all its timeouts, and now, in one of the strangest moves in the history of Rose Bowl, the Trojans run backwards to try to eat up the clock. For three straight plays they run back and away from the frantic, chasing Badgers. When, with the ball deep in their own territory, they line up to punt, there are less than 10 seconds on the clock. So time runs out, and the Trojans are victorious, 42-37, in what most people call the greatest of all Rose Bowl games. Southern Cal may have won the game, but there is no doubt that the Badgers of Wisconsin have won the hearts of the nation with one of the gamest comebacks in college football history.

ABOVE: *Wisconsin QB Ron VanderKelen about to pass to Pat Richter. VanderKelen was the hero of the game.*

RIGHT: *Fullback Roger Kurek (34) goes over from the one to score the first Badger TD. No 12 is Beathard, whose passes gained USC 401 yards and four TDs.*

W
34
26

THE PACKERS v THE COWBOYS

Ever since the American Football League was born, the establishment, the National Football League, had looked down on the upstarts. But in 1966, in exchange for $25 million, the NFL had allowed to AFL to merge with the senior league. The AFL was to continue as a separate league until 1970, when it would become the American Football Conference of the NFL. Meantime, there were to be a series of annual interleague championship games. It was the AFL's Lamar Hunt who suggested that these games be called 'Super Bowls'.

The NFLers were rooting for the Green Bay Packers to represent their league in the First Super Bowl. And the AFLers also wanted the Packers in the game, so that they could prove they could beat the best of the NFL. But in the meantime, the Packers had to beat everyone in the NFL to get into the game.

In 1965 the Packers had won their third NFL title in five years by beating the Cleveland Browns 23-12. The most interesting and controversial game of that season, however, had been an earlier contest between the Packers and the Baltimore Colts for the Western Conference title. The Colts were playing without the services of their injured star, Johnny Unitas, and on the first play the Packers also lost their ace, Bart Starr, to an injury. The game that followed was a bitter, even-handed contest. Late in the fourth quarter, with the Colts leading 10-7, the Packers' Don Chandler attempted a fieldgoal from the Colts' 22. Many spectators thought the ball went wide, but field judge Jim Tunney ruled it good, and the game went into overtime as a 10-10 tie. Four times the teams traded punts, until at last the Packers managed to fight their way down to the Colts' 18. From there Chandler kicked the winning fieldgoal, giving the game to the Packers 13-10. It had been the longest NFL game in history, and so much residual argument swirled about Chandler's first goal that the NFL rules committee was obliged to lengthen the height of goal posts by 20 feet in future games.

LEFT: *Millionaire Lamar Hunt, founder of the AFL. When the AFL and NFL began their merger in 1966 he proposed a playoff game, to be called the 'Super Bowl.'*

BELOW LEFT: *Vying to represent the NFL in the Super Bowl were Green Bay and Dallas. Here, Cowboy Bob Lilly.*

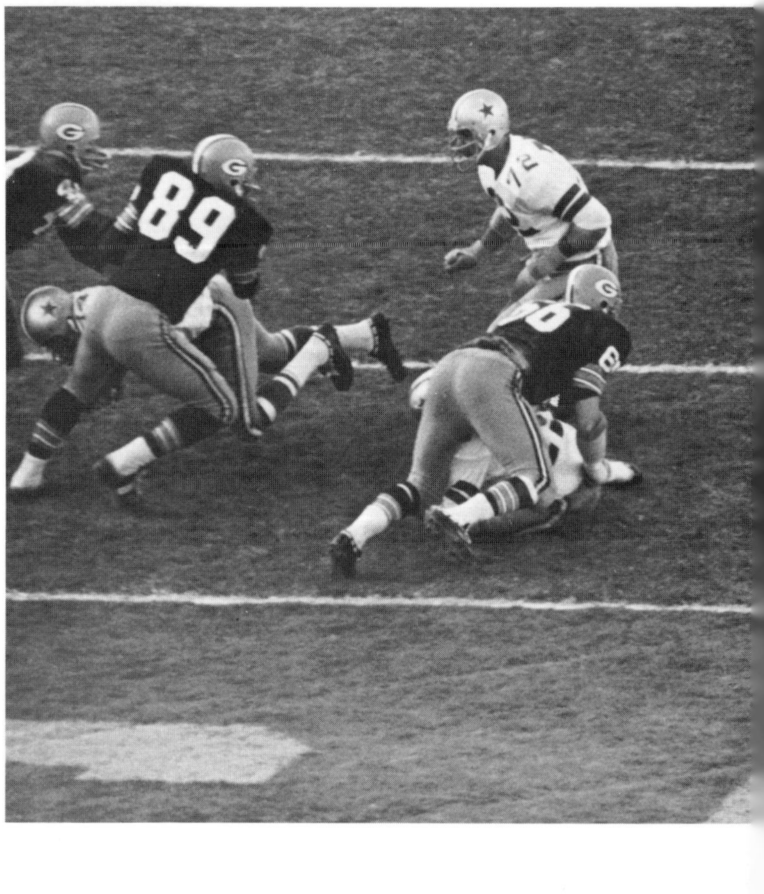

With everyone across the country assuming that the Packers would also win the 1966 NFL title, the only thing left was for the Packers to do it. The 1966 edition of Vince Lombardi's Green Bay team rivaled that of 1961 as the greatest professional team ever. With each season Bart Starr had improved, and the Packers' offensive thrust had slowly shifted from the power running game of Taylor and Hornung to the passing of Starr. Their defense was even better than in 1961, although many of the players were the same. But Herb Adderley, who was a rookie on the '61 team, was now the best defensive back in the game. Ray Nitschke had only gotten better and was rated the top middle linebacker in football, while Willie Davis was a perennial All Pro at defensive end. And the great offensive line was still intact, with Ken Bowman replacing Jim Ringo at center. In truth, Lombardi had a jewel of a team, and the Packers sliced through the Western Conference with 12 wins and only two losses in 14 games. The two losses were by a total of four points.

The Eastern Conference champions were, for the first time, the Dallas Cowboys. For a couple of years the pundits had said that the powerful young Cowboys were the team of the future, and in 1966, they finally proved the pundits right. The Cowboys presented the Packers with a unique challenge. They had what was called 'the Doomsday Defense,' led by the best defensive tackle in the game, Bob Lilly. On offense the Cowboys featured the long passing game, with Don Meredith throwing bombs to Bob Hayes, one of the world's fastest humans.

The two teams meet in the Cotton Bowl in Dallas on 1 January 1967, and before the fans could get seated the Packers scored when Bart Starr hit Elijah Pitts on a halfback flare. Disaster struck Dallas again when they fumbled the opening kickoff and Jim Grabowski, the Packers' high-priced rookie fullback, picked up the ball and scampered into the Dallas end zone. Green Bay-14, Dallas-0.

A young team such as Dallas, facing a team as dominant as the Packers, should have folded after that. But the Cowboys are for real. They come back and tie the score as both Dan Reeves and Don Perkins score on runs off the vaunted Packers defense. In the second quarter Starr hits Carroll Dale with a 51-yard bomb, and the Packers go ahead by seven. Then Don Meredith gets Dallas close enough for a fieldgoal and at the half, the Packers lead by only four.

In the third quarter Starr hits Boyd Dowler on a crossing pattern, and the tall receiver is flipped in the air by a cheap shot at his ankles after he had scored. Dowler's shoulder is injured, and he is replaced by the veteran Max McGee. Then the Cowboys get another fieldgoal, and as the fourth quarter begins, the Packers lead 28-20.

After an exchange of punts, Starr gets the Packers moving and caps off the drive to McGee with a 28-yard touchdown pass. But Bob Lilly bursts through the Packers' blockers and bats Don Chandler's extra point try aside. Now the Packers lead by 14, but the lead is cut to seven when Meredith takes the Cowboys the length of the field in five plays, the last a 68-yard bomb to his tight end, Frank Clarke.

The Packers' counter-offensive stalls, and when Don Chandler gets off a poor punt, the Cowboys have the ball on the Packers' 47 with a little over three minutes left. The Cowboys come

ABOVE LEFT: *In the first duel between Green Bay and Dallas in 1967 Jim Taylor (31) bursts through the Dallas line.*

LEFT: *In the Cotton Bowl game Green Bay scored twice in the first four minutes. But the Cowboys fought back. Here HB Don Reeves (30) makes Dallas's first TD.*

ABOVE: *Foreshortening makes this third-period pass from Starr (15) to Taylor (31) look like a score. In fact Green Bay never got past Dallas's 23 in the quarter.*

out throwing, and Meredith throws to Clarke deep. Tom Brown, the Packers' safety, grabs Clarke. Pass interference! Now the Cowboys have the ball on the Packers' two with two minutes to go.

The 70,000 Cowboys fans are standing, roaring their support. On first down Reeves gets only one yard. Next, Meredith passes into the end zone, but the Cowboys are flagged for an offside penalty. Now the Cowboys have second down and goal to go from their six. Meredith tries a pass, but Dan Reeves can't catch it. Now it is third and goal, and the old stands in the Cotton Bowl are rocking so hard some fear they'll collapse.

Meredith fires to Pettis Norman, but he catches the ball on the two and is tackled by Tom Brown. Cowboys' fourth and 45 seconds to go. The Packers' defense huddles, and Dave Robinson, their fine outside linebacker, tells his teammates that 'we've come too far to let them score.'

Meredith calls for a roll-out option pass. He fakes to the fullback and rolls to his right. If the defensive halfback drops back to cover the receiver, Meredith has a pulling guard in front of him and will run it in. If the defensive back comes up, Meredith will pass. With the snap of the ball, Dave Robinson guesses what Meredith will do. He slaps away the block of the receiver who was supposed to seal him and sprints right at Meredith, getting past Meredith's blocker. Robinson grabs the Cowboys' quarterback by his left arm, but Meredith has the ball in his right hand and throws into the end zone.

Tom Brown, the safety who had been burned by the Cowboys twice, sees Robinson grab Meredith and sees the wobbling pass coming to the end zone. Brown leaves his man and quickly cuts in front of a Dallas receiver to intercept the ball. Brown, a one-time first baseman with the Washington Senators, hugs the ball to his chest, knowing he's never made a more important catch in his life. Green Bay has won 34-27, and now they are free to go on to Pasadena to meet the AFL champion in history's first Super Bowl.

THE FIRST SUPER BOWL

After their thrilling victory over the Cowboys for the 1966 NFL title, the Green Bay Packers journeyed west to play the AFL champions in the first game of what was soon to become pro football's annual blockbuster. It was only fitting that in this first interleague championship game the Packers would be playing the team owned by the man who had both founded the AFL and coined the game's name, the Super Bowl. Lamar Hunt's Kansas City Chiefs had decisively defeated the Buffalo Bills in Buffalo on the same day that Green Bay played the Cowboys. The Kansas City Chiefs had dominated the Bills and had shown that they had both plenty of firepower and a formidable defense. Their quarterback, Len Dawson, was, in fact, an old NFLer who had played backup in the older league and had jumped to the AFL when it was formed. Their best runner was a Heisman Trophy winner, Mike Garrett of Southern Cal, and they had an excellent receiver in Otis Taylor. But it was the Chiefs' defense that made them so dangerous. At one defensive tackle was the huge, mean Buck Buchanan, and the Chiefs claimed two of the best linebackers in the AFL in Bobby Bell and E J Holub. The Chiefs also had a defensive back named Fred Williamson, a flamboyant character who wore white shoes on the football field long before Joe Namath and who gave himself the purposely menacing sobriquet 'The Hammer'.

The two leagues had agreed to allow both NBC and CBS to televise the first Super Bowl game. The media hype that the two networks put forth made the thing seem more like the War of the Worlds than just a football game. Over a thousand newspapermen converged on Los Angeles and on the two camps where the Packers and Chiefs trained. To Vince Lombardi, the season was already completed. His quarrels had been with the Bears, Lions, Colts and Cowboys. Neither he nor his players

LEFT: *In 1967 Green Bay beat Kansas City in history's first Super Bowl. Here Chiefs QB Len Dawson (16) fades back.*

BELOW: *Packer defenders Kostelnik (77), Jordan (74), Aldridge (82) and Caffey (60).*

knew anything about the Chiefs, had never even scouted them and felt no animosity towards them. Lombardi hadn't wanted or needed this game and was at something of a loss to know how to motivate his team.

Hank Stram, his counterpart in Kansas City, had the opposite problem. He had to get his team to stop being awed by the fact they they were playing the Green Bay Packers. Like most of the country, the Kansas City Chiefs had often seen the Packers on television, and the names of the Packers were more familiar to them than the names of some of their opponents in the AFL. Stram had to get them down to earth and convince them that they could indeed beat the legendary Packers. Stram knew his club could move the ball, and he felt his 'stacked' defense could stop Taylor and the other Packers runners, but he still didn't know what to do about Bart Starr.

When the Packers arrived in Santa Barbara, they were greeted by thousands of fans. They were also greeted by a newspaper headline that gave Lombardi some ammunition to get his players interested in the game. Fred Williamson, 'The Hammer,' had been bragging to the press that he personally would knock out Carroll Dale and Boyd Dowler if they dared to run a pass pattern in his area. Williamson claimed he had broken thirty helmets during the season with his famous hammer blows. So during practice, whenever Starr or Bratkowski threw passes to a receiver, as the receiver caught the pass Herb Adderley or Willie Wood would touch him on the helmet and holler, 'the Hammer gets number 31,' or 'number 32' or whatever. If the Packers were tight, it didn't show.

On the day of the game, Max McGee and Paul Hornung walked from the resort to the waiting bus. Hornung knew he wouldn't play. In the Bears game, earlier in the season, Hornung had again hurt his shoulder as he plunged into the end zone for a touchdown, and his pinched nerve hadn't healed. Lombardi was afraid that if he got hit again, he'd suffer permanent disability. McGee, on the other hand was in his 13th season and had only caught five passes in this season. In the Packers' film sessions McGee had studied the Chiefs' defensive backs and was convinced he could beat them, but he didn't know if he'd get the chance. As they walked to the bus, McGee said to Hornung, 'If Boyd(Dowler) gets hurt, I don't know how long these old legs will last.'

Both television networks had brought most of the people in the New York office to Los Angeles. At the Bowl there were three marching bands, crates filled with pigeons and two 'astronauts' flying around the stadium on jet propelled air bikes. There were 40,000 red, blue and white balloons and more movie stars than at the Academy Awards. After all the hype, the game was a great relief.

Like a couple of heavyweight fighters, the Packers and the Chiefs felt each other out. On the Packers' first series, Boyd Dowler tried to block down on the Chiefs' linebacker. When the play ended, so did Dowler's appearance in Super Bowl I. He had re-injured the shoulder he had hurt in the Dallas game and had to be taken out. In came 35-year-old Max McGee, a pro when most of the Chiefs were in grammer and high school. After an exchange of punts, the Packers began to move. Starting on their own 20, the Packers, behind two Starr passes, moved 36 yards into Kansas City territory. Then he hit Carroll Dale with a pass in front of The Hammer. Williamson delivered his hammer blow, but nothing happened. On the next play Starr sensed a blitz by the Chiefs and called a post pattern for McGee. As the Chiefs blitzed, the Packers picked them off, and McGee ran downfield, cut to the post and Starr hit him over the middle. McGee made a great one-handed catch and waltzed into the end zone. Chandler's kick made it Packers-7, Chiefs-0.

In the second quarter the Chiefs' offense came to life. Dawson would roll right or left to get away from the Packers' rush and get more time to find the receivers. This seemed to confuse the

ABOVE: *The Packers' Bart Starr prepares to pass. In all he completed 16 of 23 for 250 yards and two TDs.*

LEFT: *KC's Dawson waits for the snap. He played a good game, but the Chiefs weren't in a class with the Packers. As Lombardi put it, 'They are a good team . . . but I'd have to say NFL football is better.'*

RIGHT: *The Packers' Bob Jeter (21) vainly tries to block a Mike Mercer fieldgoal in the first half.*

Packers, and Dawson steadily took the Chiefs downfield. He hit Otis Taylor for a 31-yard gain to the Packers' 2, then rolled out and hit his fullback, Curtis McClinton, and the Chiefs tied the score.

The Packers come right back, and on third and short, Starr pulls his favorite play. He fakes a run to Jim Taylor, drops back, spots Carroll Dale breaking past the onrushing Williamson and hits him. Dale goes 64 yards for the score, but there is a yellow flag on the turf. The touchdown is called back, but Starr isn't discouraged. He puts on a clinic for Stram and the Chiefs. Three times in the drive the Packers have third and long. Each time Starr completes the pass to keep the drive going. With first and 10 on the Chiefs' 14, Starr hands off to Jim Taylor on the famed old Lombardi sweep, and behind the blocks of Kramer and Thurston, Taylor runs over Chiefs and scores. The extra point puts the Packers ahead 14-7.

The Chiefs come back to score a fieldgoal, and at halftime the American Football league has proved it can play with the big boys. For 30 minutes the Kansas City Chiefs have held their own against the supposedly invincible Green Bay Packers. And some of the old NFL owners are getting worried. Wellington Mara had wired Lombardi that he was delighted that the Packers would be carying the banner of the NFL into the battle. Now Mara isn't so sure.

While the bands play and parade the two teams make adjustments. The Packers have established that they can pass whenever they want, but they are troubled by the Chiefs' offense. So Lombardi decides that it is time to put the heat on Len Dawson. Over on the Chiefs side, Stram is secretly delighted that his team is doing so well.But he knows that somehow they still have to stop Bart Starr.

The Packers kick off to the Chiefs, and the young AFL champions fake out the old timers with their first play, as Len Dawson runs a keeper for 15 yards and a first down. After two more runs,

the Chiefs have a third and five on their own 49. Dawson calls for the roll out, and as he takes the snap from the center, the Packers blitz. Dave Robinson comes from the left, and Lee Roy Caffey from the right. Caffey gets to Dawson just as he tries to throw, and the ball sails behind the Chiefs' receiver, Fred Arbanas, and Willie Wood picks it off and races for the Chiefs' goal. Only Mike Garrett's speed prevents a touchdown: He tackles Wood on the Chiefs' five. On the next play, Starr sends Elijah Pitts behind the blocking of tackle Bob Skoronski, and he walks into the end zone. Packers-21, Chiefs-10.

It is all but over. After two more touchdowns by McGee and Pitts the Packers lead 35-10. The Chiefs' defense is now thoroughly shut down, and so with five minutes to go in the game, Lombardi pulls Starr, Taylor and Pitts and brings in his prize rookies, Donny Anderson at halfback and Jim Grabowski at fullback. He tells quarterback Zeke Bratkowski to keep it on the ground. He doesn't want the Packers to run the score too much higher.

Following his instructions, Bratkowski runs the ball. On second and 10 he calls for the Lombardi Sweep to the right. With Donny Anderson carrying the ball they head right at Fred Williamson. When the play is over, all the players get up except one. There in a heap lies The Hammer. Over on the Packers' bench there are some good-natured jibes about The Hammer being nailed, and later, in the press conference, Lombardi drives in the final nail. Someone asks him how come it took the Packers so long to get to The Hammer. Lombardi smiles and says in a quiet voice, 'It was the only time he tried to make a tackle.'

Lamar Hunt had dubbed this game 'the most important professional football ever played.' Well, maybe. Certainly it was the most publicized game played until then, and certainly the charming Mr Hunt had helped put $15,000 in each Packer's pocket, the winner's share of Super Bowl I. But more important to the Packers was the fact they they had just won their second NFL title in a row. Now they had a chance to win three in a row, something that had never happend in the National Football League since the creation of the conferences in 1933. Winning the Super Bowl was nice, the winners share was fine, but they had a new mission.

LEFT: *Green Bay fullback Elijah Pitts (22) runs to daylight. Pitts had a good day, scoring two of the Packers' five TDs. Later, Chiefs defensive end Jerry Mays would say, 'The Packers beat us in the first half, but their reputation did it in the second.'*

THE GREEN BAY PACKERS' THIRD NFL TITLE

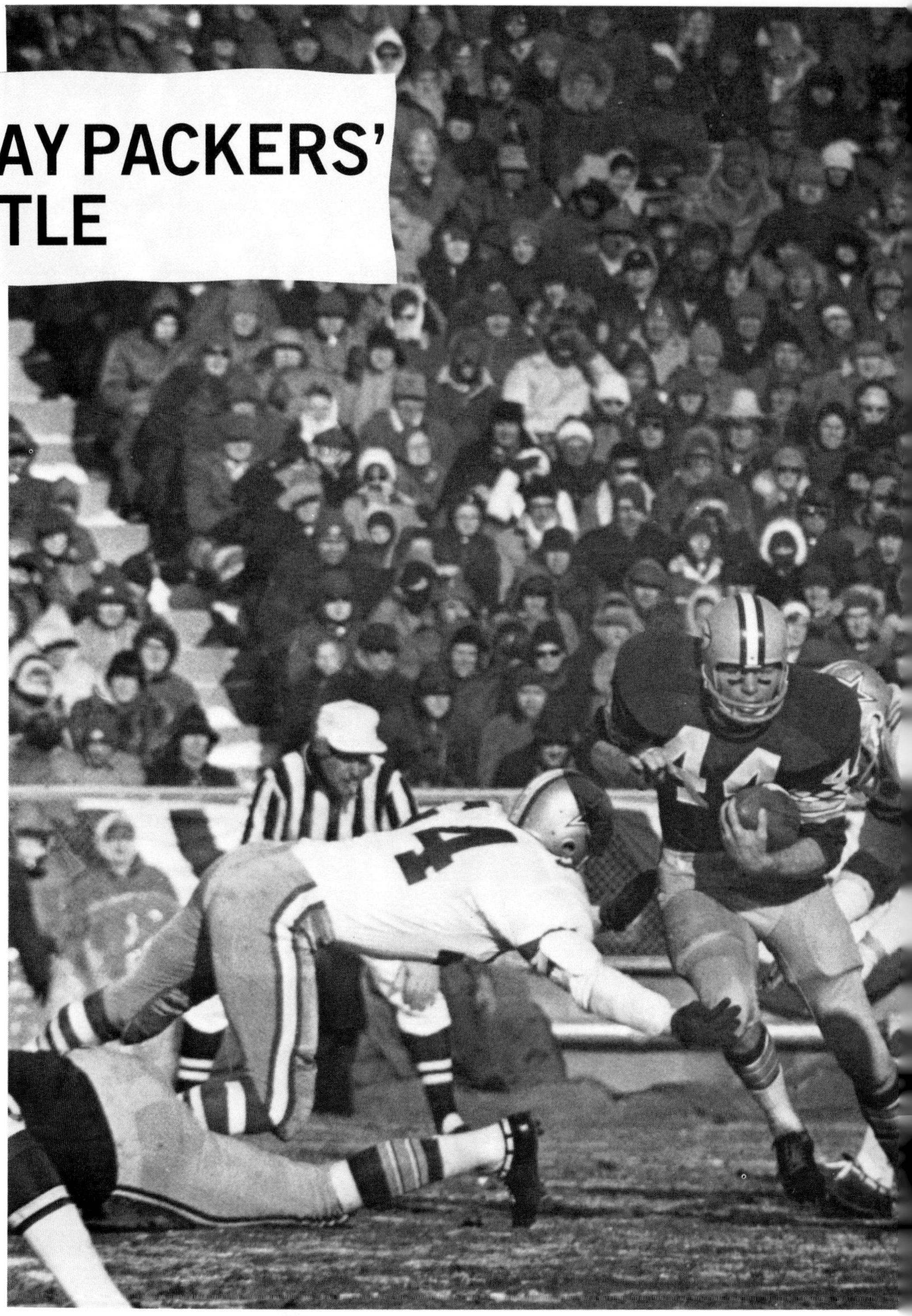

When the Green Bay Packers assembled at their training camp in the summer of 1967, and Vince Lombardi recited the names of the great teams of the post-1933 era that had failed to win three straight NFL titles, the Packers at least knew they were in august company. The Chicago Bears could have done it in 1942, but they lost 14-6 to the Washington Redskins. The Philadelphia Eagles could have done it in 1950, but they didn't even make the title game. The Detroit Lions could have set the record in 1954, but they were clobbered by the Cleveland Browns 56-10. Then the Browns gave it a shot, winning again in 1955 but finishing fourth and out of the title picture in 1956. Then the Baltimore Colts and Johnny Unitas won two in a row in 1958 and 1959 but finished third to the Packers in 1960.

Actually, the team that had had the best chance to win three in a row was the Green Bay Packers. In 1960 the Packers had lost their first NFL title game to the Eagles, a team they should have beaten easily. Lombardi's team won again in 1961 and 1962, but in 1963, although the Packers won 11 games, lost only two and tied one, the Bears won 10, lost one and tied three. Back then ties didn't count in the standings, so Chicago won the Western Conference title on the basis of percentage points.

The Packers went into the 1967 season heavily favored to win their title, but things had changed since 1966, and during the season these changes would produce conditions that would call on all the strength and motivation Vince Lombardi commanded. The NFL had expanded, putting a team in Atlanta in 1966 and another in New Orleans in 1967. These teams were stocked with veterans whom the other teams in the NFL had left unprotected. One, taken by the New Orleans team, was Paul Hornung. Lombardi had had an oral agreement with Saints' management that Hornung would be passed over, so that he could finish his career in Green Bay. Lombardi knew that the pinched nerve in Hornung's shoulder meant that he'd never really play again, but the new owner of the Saints, a rich young man named John Mecom, had wanted the glamorous Golden Boy on his roster, and Mecom's money got him.

Also missing from the Packers' 1967 team was their great fullback, Jim Taylor. Taylor was a free agent, and when he went to negotiate his contract with Lombardi, he didn't get as much money as he thought he was worth. So he shopped himself around the NFL. There were no takers, since there was an unwritten law among the owners in the NFL that there would be no bidding wars for free agents. But again John Mecom struck and offered Jim Taylor a contract he couldn't turn down. Yet Mecom's joy was short-lived. Hornung failed to pass the physical and retired, and Taylor, playing behind a line that couldn't block a hat, had his worst year as a pro and retired after the Saints' first season.

Another thing made the Packers' quest for the third title more difficult. With expansion, the league had broken up into two divisions in each conference, which meant that to get to the title game, a team always had to win the conference title in a playoff game, and not outright on the basis of the best record. It was yet another rung in the Packers' ladder.

So Vince Lombardi knew he had his work cut out for him. His defense was intact, and Bart Starr was Bart Starr. To

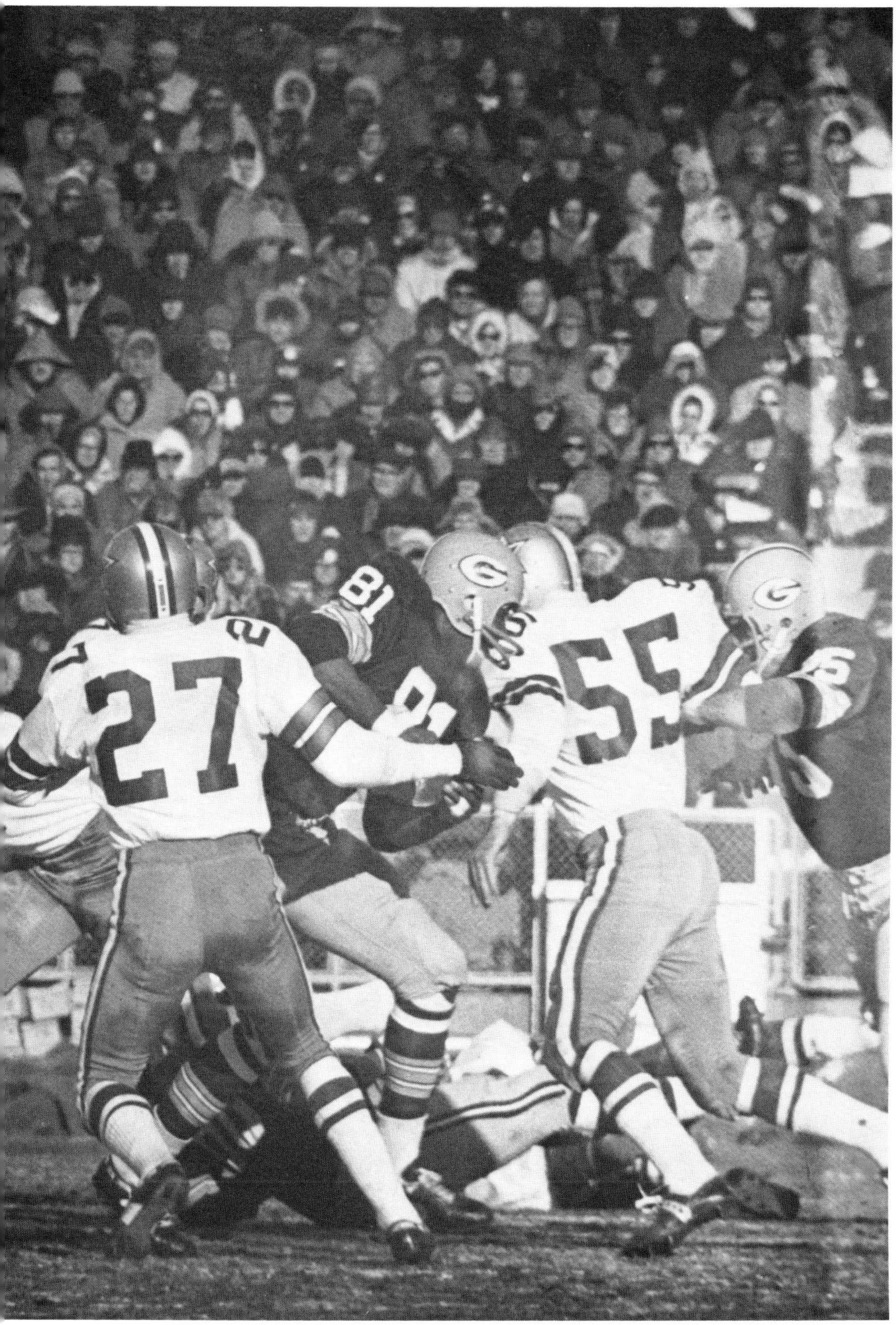

LEFT: *For the second time in 1967, on 31 December, Green Bay and Dallas played for the championship. The temperature was −13° in a 15-mph wind. Here, Packer halfback Don Anderson (44) plunges nine yards through the Dallas line.*

replace Paul Hornung and Jim Taylor, he had Elijah Pitts, who had played well for Hornung when the Golden Boy went down in the Bears game last year. The replacement for Taylor was Jim Grabowski, a taller and faster fullback, but without Taylor's hammering power. Also, Donny Anderson was almost as versatile as Hornung, and Lombardi had a rookie speed-burner in Travis Williams. The offensive line was still his pride and joy, and there were All Pros Forrest Gregg and Jerry Kramer on the right side and Ken Bowman at center, with Fuzzy Thurston at left guard and Bob Skoronski at left tackle to complete his veteran line. The receivers were the same as in Super Bowl I. Yes, this was a powerhouse, fully capable of winning the elusive third in a row.

There never has been a game like it. On 31 December 1967 the Dallas Cowboys, confident and ready, met the Green Bay Packers at Lambeau Field in Green Bay. At kickoff, the wind was blowing at 15 mph, and the temperature was 13° below zero! Even for northern Wisconsin, this was unbelievable. Before the season, Lombardi had consulted agronomists and engineers at the University of Wisconsin about lining the field in Green Bay with some kind of heating device that would keep the field dry and playable in the cold and snow of Green Bay. They had dug up Lambeau Field during the summer and installed a series of electrical grids that lay about six inches below ground. When the cold came, all the Packers had to do was throw a switch and the electrical current under the turf would thaw the ground above. Lombardi was almost as proud of that grid as he was of his football team.

When the Packers' groundkeepers heard that the temperature during the game would be below zero, they decided to put the tarp over the field for added protection. When the groundkeepers checked the field early on Sunday morning, it seemed perfect. The grass beneath the tarp was firm and solid. But on the day of the game disaster struck. Although putting the tarp over the field kept the field dry, the heat from the grids had caused condensation to form on the tarp. When it was removed, the water fell to the ground and quickly froze on top of the grass. The added pressure of frozen water and the bitter cold knocked out the grids. Thus the Packers and Cowboys would have to play this game of games on an icy, frozen field in below-zero temperatures. It is the highest of compliments to both teams that they played as well as they did in such appalling conditions.

The Packers jumped on top in the first quarter when Bart Starr hit Boyd Dowler with a short pass and they took a 7-0 lead. In the second quarter Starr struck again. With third and short, on Dallas's 43, Starr faked to his fullback, and when he turned to throw, there was Boyd Dowler with a five-step lead on defensive back Mel Renfro. Starr's pass settled easily into Dowler's outstretched arms, and he went all the way to the Dallas goal line. Green Bay 14.

But the Dallas Cowboys aren't playing in the title game just to provide the Packers with an opponent. In the middle of the second quarter, the famed Dallas Doomsday defense turns the game around. They start to go after Starr, and soon the Packers' star is being repeatedly crushed to the frozen ground. Late in the quarter, with the ball on his own 26, Bart Starr goes back to pass. He is blindsided by the Cowboys' defensive left end, Willie Townes, and fumbles. The loose ball is picked up by the other end, George Andrie, and he rumbles into the end zone. The Doomsday defense has put the Cowboys right back into the ballgame. Green Bay-14, Dallas-7.

LEFT: *Cowboys quarterback Don Meredith (17) takes the snap. His halfback option call in the fourth quarter produced a three-point lead for Dallas at a critical moment.*

RIGHT: *Packers quarterback Bart Starr (15) calls the play. His tactics in this game were among the finest in his fine career.*

BELOW: *Tackled by the Cowboys' Mel Renfro (20), Packer Boyd Dowler (86) falls over the line for Green Bay's second TD.*

The Dallas offense still can't get anything going, and with less than two minutes to go, Dallas is forced to punt to the Packers. The Packers' punt return man is their great free safety, Willie Wood. Lombardi has Wood catching the punts, not because he is a dangerous run-back man, but because he is so sure-handed. But in the bitter cold of Lambeau Field, Willie Wood, attempting a fair catch, sees the ball tumble from his frozen hands and the Cowboys recover. But the Cowboys still can't capitalize on this gift, and with seconds left, they kick a fieldgoal. Now it is Green Bay-14, Dallas-10. The Packers, famed for never making mistakes in key games, have given the Cowboys all their points. As the teams head for the warmth of their locker rooms, there is no question that 'old man momentum' has a Lone Star on his helmet.

In the locker room, Lombardi quietly talks to the Packers, reminding them that they still have the lead and 30 more minutes to win their title. Over in the Dallas room, Cowboys' coach Tom Landry tells his players that they are in better physical shape than the Packers and that if they can only keep the pressure on Starr, and if their offense can only get going, they'll win.

And the Cowboys take heed. In the third quarter the Doomsday Defense completely dominates Starr and the Packers' offense. In this quarter the Packers make only one first down. But the Cowboys' offenses is still being thwarted by the Packers' defense. Time after time, Willie Davis, Henry Jordan and the rest rise up to stop the Cowboys. The temperature begins to drop even more, and the Arctic winds that blow across the field bring the temperature on the field to a wind chill factor of -45°.

On the first play of the fourth quarter, Dallas finally strikes. With the ball at midfield, Dan Reeves tells quarterback Don Meredith that he thinks the halfback option play will work. Meredith calls it, and with the snap of the ball, he hands off to Reeves, who sweeps to his left. The Packers' defense comes up to stop the run, and they get burned by one of their own favorite plays, the halfback option. Cutting across the field from the right side is Lance Rentzel, and he gathers in Reeves's pass at the Packers' goal. Dallas-17, Green Bay-14.

Now the game becomes one of survival. The hands and toes of the players are numb with cold. Neither team can move the ball, and the 50,000 spectators in the stands are quiet. Every once in a while a lone voice will yell out, 'Lets go Pack,' but most are just sitting there, fearful that they are watching the end of the dynasty. Even with the below-zero weather, not a person has left the stadium.

The Packers' defense forces a Dallas punt, and when Willie Wood catches it and returns nine yards, the ball is on their 32 with 5:04 left in the game. The temperature on the scoreboard now reads – 16°. On the sideline Lombardi and Starr talk, and when it is time for Starr to go out to join his teammates, he looks at his coach nods and trots out to the huddle. An eerie quiet descends on Lambeau Field as the Packers line up against the Cowboys' defense, a defense that has kept them without a rushing or passing first down in the whole second half. They have 68 yards to go.

Lombardi and Starr had agreed that the Packers shouldn't try for a long gain, but should try to take advantage of whatever the Dallas defense gives them. Thus far, it has been very little. But now perhaps the miserable field conditions may favor the offense.

Starr fades to pass, and as the Cowboys rush him, he dumps a little swing pass off to Donny Anderson that gains six. Then Chuck Mercein bounces around right end for seven, and the Packers have their first first down in the second half. To keep the Dallas secondary aware of his wide receivers, Starr calls a slant over the middle to Boyd Dowler. The tall receiver catches the ball for a 13-yard gain to the Dallas 42. When the Cowboys tackle Dowler they fling him bodily to the hard ground, and Dowler literally spins on his head on the frozen field. Yet he gets up and joins the huddle, and the fans stand and cheer.

But the cheers turn to groans as Anderson is dropped for a nine-yard loss. Second and 19, and Starr quickly goes to work. Rather than try to get it all back with one pass, he uses his backs flaring out of the backfield, keeping the Dallas' linebackers in with fakes to one or the other back. A pass to Anderson gets 12, and with third and seven at the Dallas 30, Starr hits Chuck Mercein for a 19-yard gain, a first down, and as Mercein goes out of bounds on the Cowboys' 11, the clock stops. Fifty thousand fans are standing and screaming their lungs out. Who cares if they are suffering from the cold?

With 1:11 left, Bart Starr makes a call that will forever stamp him as one of the great field generals in football history. The strength of the Packers' running attack for years has been the Lombardi sweep. Now with Taylor and Hornung gone, there are only Anderson and whoever the fullback is to run it. The success of the sweep depends on keeping the defense from penetrating until the back turns upfield. The strength of the Dallas defense is Bob Lilly, whose strength and quickness make him the ideal defender to stop the sweep. Five or six times during the game, the Packers have run the sweep to the right, with Anderson carrying the ball. Every time the Cowboys have stopped it for little or no gain, usually because of Lilly's quick pursuit.

With first down on the Dallas 11, Starr tells the Packers what he intends to do, and Jerry Kramer remembers thinking, 'What a great call!' The Packers line up in the formation for the sweep, and with the snap of the ball, Gale Gillingham, the left guard over whom Lilly is playing, pulls to his right as he always does on the sweep. Starr pivots and starts to hand the ball to Anderson. Lilly has followed Gillingham through the hole he created when he pulled, and he goes for Anderson, but Starr has slipped the ball to Mercein, and in a flash the fullback is

through the open spot where Lilly should have been. He gets to the Dallas three before being tackled.

On the next play, with 54 seconds left, Starr hands off to Anderson who gains two for a first down. The ball now rests on the Cowboys' one-yard line with 30 seconds left. One yard to go, the clock is winding down, and the Packers have only one time-out left. They try a dive play, but the Cowboys stop it. With 20 seconds on the clock, the Packers try to wedge Anderson in again, but he slips on the frozen field and almost fumbles. Starr quickly calls their last timeout and goes over to the sidelines to talk to Vince Lombardi.

Sixteen seconds to go. The ball on the one yard line and the Packers are out of timeouts. Should they kick the sure fieldgoal and tie the game so as to go into overtime? That's the smart play. Vince Lombardi is a conservative coach, always reducing the risks, and everyone thinks that the Packers will surely kick.

But Lombardi has something else in mind. In the huddle, Starr calls another wedge play, in which Anderson is to run behind the drive blocks of Gregg and Kramer. Up to the line they come. They know they have to score, because there isn't enough time on the clock to get the field goal team out if they fail. The Cowboys dig in as best they can, for by now the goal line is solid ice. Ken Bowman snaps the ball, and the two lines collide. Kramer drives on Jethro Pugh, the huge Dallas tackle, as Gregg buries Willie Townes, the end. Starr keeps the ball and follows Gregg and Kramer . . . into the end zone! Green Bay-20, Dallas-17.

LEFT: *The game-winning final Packer score. With only 16 seconds left, Starr, instead of kicking for a tie, ran it over for a TD.*

BELOW: *Vince Lombardi and Packer defensive coach Phil Bengtson watch as Starr makes the winning score.*

Lambeau Field erupts, and on the sideline, Lombardi is raising his arms in the touchdown signal. Chandler's extra point is good. The Packers kick off with 13 seconds left, and two Don Meredith passes fall harmlessly to the ground. It is over. The Green Bay Packers have won their third straight National Football League crown, the fifth in seven years.

In the wild locker room after the game, the press asked Starr about the call. 'The decision to go for it was Coach Lombardi's,' he said. 'There never was any discussion of kicking the fieldgoal.' Starr also admitted that when he called the wedge play, he didn't tell the team that he would keep it. It was supposed to go to Chuck Mercein, but Starr knew that Anderson had slipped on the previous play, and if Mercein slipped now, they'd never score. So he just kept it himself.

As the years have gone by, many have come to put the 'Ice Bowl' game on a par with, or even ahead of, the 1958 'Sudden Death' classic between the Giants and Colts. All things considered – what was at stake, the bitter conditions, the great defense standing in their way – the Green Bay Packers' performance in those last five minutes probably do make the 'Ice Bowl' the greatest pro game ever played.

THE JETS COME TO SUPER BOWL III

After two humiliating losses to the Green Bay Packers and the NFL, the American Football League badly wanted to win a Super Bowl. The fans of the older circuit looked down on the newer league, and they pointed to the results of the first two Super Bowls to prove their point. Fans of the AFL retorted that obviously the other teams in the NFL couldn't beat the Packers either, but that argument fell on deaf ears. The AFL needed a miracle, and they got one.

As the 1968 season swung into November, it was obvious that Ray Nitschke's statement that 'the players are the reason the Packers win' was not the whole truth. They trailed in their division, and by mid-November, when the Baltimore Colts came to Green Bay, the Colts were undefeated, even though Johnny Unitas was injured. If the Packers were going to get back into the title chase, they had to beat the Colts. But in a typical Colts/Packers game, the bitterly fought contest swung to the Colts. The 50,000 fans stood and sang 'Auld Lang Syne.' In his special box along press row, Vince Lombardi cried. The Packers' reign was over.

The new kings were the Baltimore Colts. And deservedly so. After the years of finishing second to Green Bay, they now headed for the top of the NFL. In fact, they so dominated the league in 1968 that some commentators began calling the Colts the 'greatest team in the history of the game.' After just one season?

In the American Football League, still smarting from the two losses to Green Bay, a new star had arisen and became the talk of football, at least in the New York press. 'Broadway Joe' Namath was the man, and he led a team of talented individuals against the best in the AFL. Namath had a throwing arm the envy of any who ever tried to pass a football. He was tough, playing on two damaged knees and absorbing the beating of defensive players he couldn't avoid because of his immobility. He read defenses quickly, and his passes were away so fast that defenders often couldn't get to him before he launched the ball downfield. Almost by himself, Joe Namath focused the attention of the media on the AFL.

Late in November the Jets traveled to Oakland to play the Raiders. NBC was

LEFT: *In Super Bowl III NY Jets quarterback 'Broadway Joe' Namath (12) led his team to a stunning upset over the Baltimore Colts.*

ABOVE: *Earlier in 1968 NBC cut short a Jets-Raiders game to show* Heidi. *Thus Raider Charlie Smith's (23) winning TD went unseen.*

LEFT: *Favored to win Super Bowl III by as much as 55-0, the Colts at first dominated.*

televising the game. The teams kicked off at 1 PM, Pacific Coast time, 4 PM in New York. By the time the New York clock read 7 PM, the Jets led 32-29, the Raiders had the ball on the Jets' 43 and the clock in the stadium showed 42 seconds to play. And that was the last anyone, other than those in the stadium, saw of the game.

NBC cut away from the game to run a movie, *Heidi*, and the millions who had been following the game never saw Daryle Lamonica lead the Raiders back for two touchdowns to beat the Jets in just 42 seconds!

The NBC switchboard lit up like a Christmas tree as calls from outraged fans poured in, and when they were told that the Raiders had pulled off a great come-from-behind win, the callers became even more incensed. NBC apologized, and the National Football League wrote in a rule in their contracts with the networks to the effect that, except for a national emergency such as World War III, the games would thereafter be shown until the final gun. The new rule was called the 'Heidi' Rule, of course.

As fate would have it, the Raiders and the Jets met again, this time in New York, at Shea Stadium, and this time for the AFL title and the right to get slaughtered by the awesome Baltimore Colts. The Jets won, but when they woke up the next morning to read about their victory the first thing they saw was that Jimmy 'the Greek' Snyder, a famous bookmaker from Las Vegas, had rated them 18-point underdogs in the Super Bowl. In an interview quoted in the New York papers Snyder added that if Unitas were playing for the Colts, there would be no points. 'Too many to give.'

On the night when Namath accepted the AFL's Most Valuable Player award he made a short acceptance speech. In it he told the audience, 'I guarantee you that we will win on Sunday.' When the Namath quote hit the street, NFL fans were both annoyed and amused. They didn't like Namath, or his mustache, or his white football shoes, but they had

ABOVE: *Jets coach Weeb Ewbank had prepared carefully for the game, studying film and drilling Namath on short passes.*

to admit that for him to have the audacity to guarantee a victory had finally gotten some life into what had been a dull pre-game week. Now the fans couldn't wait to see the famed Baltimore defense, led by Bubba Smith, tear Namath limb from limb. 'Kill, Bubba, Kill!'

Among all the thousands and thousand of words that poured forth from the press during the week before Super Bowl III, little attention was paid to a story that had some genuine drama. The man who owned the Baltimore Colts was a flamboyant entrepreneur named Carroll Rosenbloom. He had hired Weeb Ewbank to coach the Colts, and Ewbank had responded with two NFL titles and had kept the Colts in contention throughout the Packers' dynasty. But that wasn't good enough for Rosenbloom, and he had fired Ewbank and replaced him with Don Shula in 1963. Bitter at Rosenbloom, Weeb Ewbank took over the fortunes of the New York Jets when Sonny Werblin assumed control of the team from Harry Wismer.

Shula had taken the Colts to the NFL title game in 1964, and Rosenbloom had felt justly proud of his wisdom in canning Ewbank. But when the Browns destroyed the Colts in that championship match 27-0, Rosenbloom's love for Shula had faltered somewhat. Still, by 1968, with the Colts back on top, Rosenbloom was again feeling well disposed towards the lantern-jawed Shula, and all during the week before the game he was busy planning a huge party at his estate in Hollywood, Florida, to celebrate the Colts' victory. Over 5000 guests had been invited, and a mammoth blue-and-white tent covered his back yard. There were Colts banners and pom poms all over the tent and at each of the tables. It would be memorable.

While Rosenbloom was inviting special friends to his celebration, the man whom he had fired was studying the Colts' films. Many of the Colts had been drafted, signed and coached by Ewbank. He knew their strengths and weaknesses very well, indeed, and now the little round man whom Carroll Rosenbloom thought wasn't good enough was beginning to formulate some ideas about how the Colts might be beaten.

Meantime, Namath was still getting under the Colts' skins, this time by announcing that he thought that there were at least two or three quarterbacks in the AFL better than Earl Morrall, the Colts' star quarterback and the NFL's Most Valuable Player in 1968. What Namath had publicly said about Morrall was, in fact, privately felt by many NFL coaches. The crew-cut Morrall was good, but the feeling was that if you could get to Morrall, you could shake him up. Ewbank, studying the films, knew that if his team would follow his lead and let the Colts make mistakes, the Jets might win. But first he had to neutralize the Colts' defense.

The day of the game came up cloudy and dark, not the approved Chamber of Commerce day that Miamians brag about. The Jets had by now climbed to 20-point underdogs, despite what Namath had guaranteed. And on the Colts' first possession it looked as though 20 points wouldn't be enough. The Colts rolled down the field with ease and reached the Jets' 19. Now Morrall fired a pass to his All Pro receiver, Willie Richardson. Richardson, on a post pattern, took Morrall's pass at the goal line and promptly dropped it. The Jets then stopped an attempted run, and then Lou Michaels came in for a chip-shot fieldgoal from the 27. The snap was perfect, but the left-footed kicker squibbed the ball wide to the left, and the Jets took over on their 20.

Now the Colts got a gift when George Sauer fumbled after catching a Namath pass, and the Colts had another scoring chance on the Jets' 12. They lost it when Morrall's pass to tight end Tom Mitchell hit the receiver on the shoulder pads and bounced into the hands of Jets defensive back Randy Beverly.

Now the Jets begin to move. Ewbank had wanted the Jets to run away from Bubba Smith and towards right end Ordell Braase and linebacker Don Shinnick. The Jets' fullback, Matt Snell, is a strong, quick runner, and after taking the handoff from Namath, he feints as if he's going off tackle and then veers outside. His blockers drive Braase in and take Shinnick in the direction Snell wants to go, and he bounces outside, upfield. Three running plays by Snell, and the Jets are on their 46. On third and four, Namath drills a 14-yard pass to Sauer, and the Jets have a first down in Baltimore territory. Mixing passing with running, the Jets score from five yards out on the same Snell off-end play. The extra point makes it Jets-7, Colts-0, and if any bettor had taken the

my Orr, and Orr was the primary receiver on the play. Namath's prediction seems good as the Jets leave the field at the half, leading 7-0. And in the NBC broadcasting booth, Kurt Gowdy, the fine play-by-play man, and Paul Christman, the best color man in broadcasting, can't believe what they just saw. The Jets have been outplayed on offense, and the only reason the Jets' defense has kept them in the game is that the Colts have made so many errors. The NFL fans are puzzled and fearful. Carroll Rosenbloom is livid. So are the other NFL owners. They took the AFLers' money to let them in, but that didn't mean that they could win the title game.

LEFT: *Jet fullback Matt Snell (41) carries as Colt tackle Billy Ray Smith (74) closes in. Snell started the first Jets drive.*

BELOW: *Interceptions and fumbles contributed much to the Jets' victory. Ewbank had been counting on the Colts making mistakes, and they obliged him.*

Jets, he now leads 27-0.

The Colts revive behind a 58-yard run by Tom Matte, the erstwhile quarterback. Morrall then passes to Richardson, but the Jets' Johnny Sample, a former Colt, jumps in front of Richardson and takes the ball away for the interception.

The Colts' mistakes are beginning to pile up, and Ewbank's idea of letting the Colts hang themselves on their own mistakes is paying off. With a minute to go the Colts make their worst mistake. On a 'flea-flicker' play Morrall hands the ball off to Tom Matte. Matte heads to the right, stops and passes the ball back to Morrall, who has drifted towards the sideline. Morrall catches the ball, and there isn't a New York player within 20 yards of him. Jimmy Orr, the Colts' end, has drifted down to the goal line and is standing there, with the nearest Jets 15 yards away. Orr waves his arms, but Morrall doesn't see him. Now the Jets start coming at Morrall, but he still has plenty of time. Orr is frantically jumping up and down, and still no Jets are near him, but Morrall throws to Jerry Hill, his fullback, on the goal line. He completes the pass, not to Hill, but to the Jets' Jim Hudson, who was standing next to Hill!

Morrall has thrown his third interception. He completely missed Jim-

It doesn't get any better for Baltimore in the third period. On the first play of the second half Tom Matte fumbles, and the Jets recover. When Namath can't move, Jim Turner comes in and kicks a 33-yard fieldgoal. Jets-10, Colts-0. Three more unsuccessful series by the Colts, and Namath begins another Jets drive. Two 14-yard passes to George Sauer, who is eating Lenny Lyles alive, get the Jets near enough for another Turner fieldgoal. Jets-13, Colts-0.

After the Colts run back the Jets' kickoff, a tremendous roar greets them as they jog off the field. Running out to quarterback the Colts is Number 19,

Johnny Unitas, He hasn't played since his injury in early fall, and he is rusty. But he is the Colts' only hope now. Yet Unitas does not rally the Colts. Randy Beverly intercepts a poorly thrown pass, and Namath drives the Jets downfield. As the third quarter ends, the Jets are in position for another Turner fieldgoal. They get it, and as the darkness begins to cover the Orange Bowl, John Unitas has less than 14 minutes to bring the Colts back.

The old master begins. His passes set up the Colts' runners, and for the first time in the second half the Colts begin to get first downs. Unitas brings the Colts deep into Jets territory. But now he is faced with a fourth and long from his 20. Unitas hits Orr, and the receiver gets inside the Jets' five. Jerry Hill takes it over from the one. The Colts still have plenty of time to get back into the game. Their specialty team recovers an onside kick, and the Orange Bowl rocks in anticipation of another classic Unitas drive. When two of his passes bring the Colts to the Jets' 24, the Jets and the AFL fans begin to realize that there is still magic left in the arm of Johnny Unitas. But now the Jets defense puts back its collective ears and rush the great Johnny U. Johnny Sample tips away a sure reception by Richardson, and the pass rush forces Unitas to hurry his next throw. Finally, on fourth and long, he tries for the end zone, hoping for a score, but the ball is just too far from the lunging Orr.

TOP: *Veteran Colts QB Johnny Unitas (19) replaced Earl Morrall in the third period.*

ABOVE: *Unitas fades back. An injured right elbow interfered with his passing.*

As Unitas trots over to the Colts' bench, you can see that there is no more life in the Baltimore team. They have lost. When Namath sends Snell into the line six straight times, picking up first downs, the game is over. The gun sounds, and thousands who said it couldn't be done run on to the field to touch Joe Namath. As Joe jogs to the locker room, he raises his right index finger, signaling Number One. With this stunning upset, in a little over two hours Weeb Ewbank, Joe Namath and the rest of the New York Jets have brought parity to the game.

Namath and the Jets would never return to the Super Bowl together. But what they accomplished on the turf in the Orange Bowl that day will forever be remembered as the day the AFL came in from the cold.

The Miraculous Reception

In 1969, the year that began with the Jets' stunning Super Bowl upset of the Raiders, the Pittsburgh Steelers, long the doormat of pro football, hired a new coach. His name was Chuck Noll, and he had played for Paul Brown and had later coached under that great master. Noll's first year at the helm of the Steelers was a disaster, winning one game and losing 13. But owner Art Rooney stuck with Noll, and soon the high draft choices the Steelers were getting from all those losing seasons began to pay off. In 1972 the Steelers finally made it to the playoffs, and late in December they met the heavily favored Oakland Raiders in an American Conference playoff game. The winner would play the Miami Dolphins, champions of the American Football Conference.

The Steelers had a great defense, anchored by Mean Joe Greene, one of those first-round draft choices the Steelers had accumulated, a tackle of great quickness, strength and hostility. The Steelers' offense was led by a young, strong-armed quarterback just starting to come into his own, Terry Bradshaw, and a fullback from Penn State, Franco Harris. Just being in the playoffs was so great for the long-suffering Steelers fans that, win or lose, Three Rivers stadium in Pittsburgh was a very happy place.

The Raiders were a strong defensive team with a deserved reputation for pugnacity. On offense they had the 'Mad Bomber,' Daryle Lamonica, a veteran of the playoffs, and they were favored over the young, inexperienced Steelers. But Lamonica had come down with flu, and his passes lacked the necessary zip to get to the receivers. In the second half, therefore, the Raiders' coach John Madden substituted Kenny Stabler for the ill Lamonica. Neither team had scored in the first half, as both defenses seemed to be dominant. In a mill town such as Pittsburgh this was the fans' kind of game. The hitting was brutal on both sides.

As the sun began to set and the cold seeped into the stadium, the offenses finally began to work. Bradshaw led the Steelers deep into Raiders territory, where Roy Gerela booted an 18-yard fieldgoal for the first score, and the Steelers led 3-0. When Stabler was hit hard by the Steelers' rush, he fumbled, and Gerela kicked one from the 29. Now Pittsburgh was up 6-0, with only 3:50 minutes to play.

Ken Stabler knew he had to get something going, and on fourth and one he handed off to Charley Smith for an all-important first down. With some quick passes Stabler then brought Raiders down to the Steelers' 30. There was less than a minute and a half to go. The Steelers knew they had to stop Stabler's passing, so they called a safety blitz. When Stabler set up to pass again he found that the pressure was too great, so he suddenly rolled around

ABOVE: *In the NFL since 1933, Pittsburgh had never been in a title game until coach Chuck Noll led them to the 1972 playoff.*

LEFT: *Tackle 'Mean Joe' Greene anchored the Steeler defense in the 1972 playoff game with the Oakland Raiders.*

a rushing Steeler and found a wide-open lane to the goal line. Stabler ran the length of it, and when the extra point was kicked the Raiders led 7-6, with just 73 seconds to go.

Earlier in the game the Steelers had had the ball, fourth and one, deep in Raiders' territory. Chuck Noll had waved off the sure fieldgoal, and the Steelers had gone for the first down. The Raiders had stopped them. Now Noll stood on the sidelines berating himself for passing up that sure fieldgoal, for at this critical moment they would have been leading 9-7, instead of trailing 7-6.

The Raiders' kickoff hits the crossbar on the goalposts, so the Steelers have no runback and have to start from their own 20. Bradshaw gets them to the Raiders' 40 with two passes, but the Raiders' defense, led by defensive back Jack Tatum, swat away the next Bradshaw passes. With fourth and 10, and 22 seconds to go, Noll sends in a play. It is an over-the-middle pass to Barry Pearson. Its object is to get deep enough for a desperate fieldgoal. Up in the press box, Art Rooney slowly rises and heads for the elevators. In 40 years his team has never come so close to winning a playoff game, but he figures it is over, and he wants to be in the locker room to help console his players.

On the field, the Steelers break the huddle and come to the scrimmage line. Bradshaw takes the snap and retreats, looking for Pearson. Franco Harris has stayed in to block, but the Raiders' rush is too strong, and when Bradshaw begins to scramble away from the Raiders' rush, Harris heads downfield, waving his hands at Bradshaw.

Bradshaw ignores Harris. He sees that Pearson is covered, but then spots his halfback, John 'Frenchy' Fuqua. But Jack Tatum of the Raiders has seen Bradshaw looking at Fuqua, so when Bradshaw throws to Fuqua, the ball and Tatum arrive at the same time. Tatum gives Fuqua a wicked belt, and the ball goes flying backwards.

ABOVE: *Steeler QB Terry Bradshaw carrying. Just coming into his own in 1972, he would star in three Super Bowls.*

Also running towards Fuqua is the Steelers' Franco Harris, and he sees Tatum's hit, and his eyes bulge as the football heads directly at him. Without breaking stride Harris catches the ball and heads straight for the Raiders' goal. At the 10 he is almost tackled, but he brushes aside the attempt and scores! The last thing Bradshaw has seen, before being buried under three Raiders, is Fuqua losing the ball, so he knows nothing of Harris's catch. Underneath the pileup Bradshaw hears tremendous cheering, but he

ABOVE: *In the game's last seconds Bradshaw's pass to Fuqua bounced off him into Harris's (32) hands.*

RIGHT: *Franco Harris.*

can't figure why the Steelers' fans would be cheering. Then one of the Raiders starts swearing, and Bradshaw frees himself to witness the wildest scene he has ever viewed. Steelers are grabbing and hugging each other, and the fans are cheering crazily. Bradshaw looks at the scoreboard; it is still Oakland-7, Pittsburgh-6. He is completely baffled.

Finally one of the Steelers grabs Bradshaw and tells him of Harris's touchdown. But still the officials haven't signaled. If the ball bounced off Fuqua and did not touch Tatum, then the ball is dead. If both touched the ball, the touchdown stands. For what seems an eternity, the officials discuss it. Pat Harder and Adrian Burke, both former NFL stars, are part of the officiating crew, and they assure Referee Fred Swearington that the play is legal. So up goes Swearington's arms. Touchdown! The Steelers win!

Art Rooney, standing by the elevators hears the noise, and when a vendor runs up to him shouting 'You won it! You won it!' Rooney just stares at him and says, 'You've got to be kidding.'

It has come to be known as the 'Miraculous Reception.' To this day, Raiders fans and many officials swear that Tatum never touched the ball, but Art Rooney, a deeply religious man, feels that his 40 years of faith in and prayer for a Steelers' victory were finally answered. And after that play, who's to disagree?

MIAMI'S UNBEATEN SEASON 1972-73

In the same season that contained the Steelers' wondrous finish the Miami Dolphins were on their way to an accomplishment never before matched in pro football. In 1972, three years after he had taken a losing franchise and turned it around, Don Shula wanted to win the 1973 Super Bowl VII more than any single accomplishment in his long and successful coaching career.

In just two years Shula had brought the Dolphins to Super Bowl VI, but there they had run into a Dallas Cowboy team more than ready to achieve the success so many had predicted for them. When the Dolphins lost, critics had said that Shula might be able to get his team to a title game, but he couldn't win it. They cited the time in 1964 when Shula was coaching the Baltimore Colts and, although heavily favored, lost to the Cleveland Browns 27-0. And, of course, they reminded people that it was Shula who was coaching the Colts when they were beaten in pro football's greatest upset by the New York Jets in Super Bowl III. Leading the chorus of critics was Carroll Rosenbloom, Shula's former boss when he was with the Colts. Rosenbloom had taken personally the Colts' loss to the Jets and blamed it all on Shula. Losing to the Dallas Cowboys in the 1972 Super Bowl had only fanned the fire that burned deeply in Don Shula. He tried to pay no heed to the critics, but down deep he knew that if he didn't win a Super Bowl soon, Carroll Rosenbloom and the rest would succeed in having him labeled a loser.

LEFT: *Don Shula came to the Dolphins in 1970. By 1972 he had them playing in the Super Bowl. When they lost that game Shula's critics said it proved he couldn't work under pressure.*

His players knew of the unfair criticism that was heaped on their coach, and to a man they vowed that they would return to the Super Bowl and win it. The team that Don Shula had created was now fully developed. At quarterback he had Bob Griese, whom he had patiently been grooming into a player worthy of being ranked with the great Bart Starr. Griese's backfield mates were Larry Csonka, the prototype of a power fullback, Jim Kiick, a hard-running and versatile halfback, Eugene 'Mercury' Morris, mercury-quick and strong.

The Dolphins' defense did not feature any household names, so someone dubbed them the 'No-name Defense.' After all, the Minnesota Vikings had the 'Purple People Eaters' and the Rams had the 'Fearsome Foursome' and the Cowboys had the 'Doomsday Defense,' so why not the 'No Names'?

As the season progressed, the Dolphins made quick work of their opponents. But in the fifth game, Bob Griese went down with an injury. Shula looked to his bench, and ready to play for him was Earl Morrall. He was 38 years old, but Shula had great confidence in him. When the Colts had lost to the Jets in Super Bowl III, many had blamed Morrall for the upset. But Shula never once criticized his quarterback, and when Shula went to Miami, he brought Morrall along to help develop Bob Griese. Now, even with Griese out, the Dolphins continued to win.

They had a close call against Minnesota, pulling out a win on a Garo Yepremian fieldgoal with time almost out. They won by only one point over the Buffalo Bills. And they clinched the title by narrowly beating the Jets 28-24. But in the playoffs, they were able to dispose of both the Cleveland Browns and the Pittsburgh Steelers. So when they went to Los Angeles to play in Super Bowl VII, the Miami Dolphins had won all 16 games of the regular season and the playoffs. Now they had just one more to win to get Don Shula his championship and to complete an undefeated, untied season.

Surprisingly, the undefeated Dolphins entered the game as three-point underdogs. The team they would face had its own nickname, 'The Over-the-Hill Gang.' The Washington Redskins were a colorful group of players gathered from all over the NFL. Their coach, George Allan, whose motto was 'today is the future,' had traded draft choices to get veterans whom he thought could make the Redskins immediate winners. And he was correct. Their strength was their defense, a hard-hitting group that was tough against both runners and passers.

The Redskins had suffered a serious blow when their great quarterback, Sonny Jurgensen, had injured his heel in a game against the Giants and was lost to the team for the rest of the season. But going into this game, it would be Billy Kilmer at quarterback, and Kilmer was a winner. His passes may have looked like flailing ducks, but somehow he always brought the Redskins through. Behind Kilmer was one of football's best runers, Larry Brown. He had been a rookie when Vince Lombardi had coached the Redskins in 1969-70. Lombardi had noticed that Brown didn't get off on the snap of the ball, was always a split second too slow. He took the rookie aside to talk to him and discovered that Larry Brown had suffered a childhood disease that had impaired his hearing. So all Lombardi did was put a hearing aid in Larry Brown's helmet, and suddenly the Redskins had a superstar.

Since the game was being played in Los Angeles, there was a great deal of support for the Redskins, since they represented the NFC, the conference the LA Rams were in. The owner of the Los Angeles Rams was, in fact, none other than Carroll Rosenbloom. He had swapped his Baltimore franchise with Robert Irsay, owner of the Rams. So when Don Shula brought his Dolphins into Tinseltown, there was Carroll Rosenbloom making snide remarks about him to the LA press. The press was happy to play up the feud between the two, and some reporters openly predicted that the pressure on Shula would cost the Dolphins the game.

George Allan was also returning to Los Angeles. He had coached the Rams to some of their best seasons in the mid-60s and early 70s, but his free-spending ways had resulted in their parting company. Now George Allan, who had never won an NFL title while with the Rams, was returning with the Washington Redskins, favored to win. He, too, was full of caustic comments about Shula.

In the end, it was Allan, rather than

LEFT: *Miami coach Don Shula used veteran Earl Morrall (15) to back up and help develop regular QB Bob Griese.*

RIGHT: *Among Shula's assets entering Super Bowl VII was 240-lb power back Larry Csonka (39).*

Shula, who was most affected by the pressure. He saw spies everywhere when the team practiced. He fussed over his players like a mother hen. When the players' wives arrived, Allan was quoted as saying 'They'll have their whole lives together, but there is only one Super Bowl. I wish the plane had stopped in Chicago.' By the time Game Day rolled around, George had the Redskins so tense that they were in the worst imaginable psychological shape for the game.

The Dolphins, on the other hand, played with coolness and intensity. Bob Griese took the Dolphins downfield for a score in the first quarter. Mixing runs and judicious use of his passes, Griese brought the Dolphins to the Redskins' 28. Griese had a future Hall of Famer in Paul Warfield as one receiver, and the Redskins double-teamed him. They also put their best

LEFT: *Redskin QB Billy Kilmer (17) about to pass. Unfortunately, Miami's 'no-name defense' left him few receivers.*

RIGHT: *Miami QB Bob Griese (12) was not a flamboyant player, but he was a cool and brilliant play-caller.*

BELOW: *Washington's fine back Larry Brown (43) had a slight hearing disability and wore a hearing aid in his helmet.*

ABOVE: *Middle linebacker Nick Buoniconti (85) set up Miami's second TD when he intercepted a Kilmer pass.*

RIGHT: *Redskins coach George Allan watches Miami win the game.*

pass defender, Pat Fischer, on Howard Twilley, Griese's other receiver. Twilley wasn't fast but had good moves. When Griese dropped back to pass, he pump faked at Warfield. Twilley, driving downfield, feinted towards the post, and when Fischer moved that way. Twilley drove past him into the end zone to catch Griese's perfect pass. He had turned Fischer completely around.

Kilmer tried to bring the Redskins back, but he was intercepted by middle linebacker Nick Buoniconti, who ran it back to the Redskins' 27. Now the Dolphins, behind that great line, powered the ball towards the Redskins' goal. Jim Kiick shot into the end zone from two yards out, and the Dolphins led 14-0.

For most of the rest of the game, the only excitement was generated by the antics of George Allan on the sidelines. Nothing the Redskins attempted worked, and even though their defense was controlling the Dolphins, the 'Skins couldn't make any offensive headway. Late into the fourth quarter the Dolphins began a time-killing drive downfield. The Redskins stiffened, and with less than five minutes to go, Shula decided to go for a fieldgoal to put the game out of reach. In came Garo Yepremian, and now the Super Bowl began to get exciting.

The little Cypriot stands at the 32-yard line and gets ready for his 42-yard attempt. The ball is snapped, and Garo steps forwards and kicks. As he looks up he sees the ball coming right back to him! Bill Brundige, the Redskins' huge tackle, has sliced through the Dolphins' blocking and has batted the ball right back to Garo. He catches it and looks at the ball as if it were a time bomb, for Yepremian realizes that the onrushing horde of Redskins are all after him. He lifts the ball over his head, in a sort of parody of Bob Griese, and tries to throw it. The ball wobbles through the air and flutters into the hands of Mike Bass of the Redskins. Bass knows very well what to do with a football, and he heads downfield, right past an apopletic Don Shula.

With the score now 14-7, George Allan and his Redskins are back in the game. The break they have been waiting for has finally arrived. But they still have to stop Griese, and that is not an easy thing to do. Griese takes the Dolphins to one first down after another. The Redskins use all their time-outs trying to stop the clock, but when they finally force the Dolphins to punt, they get the ball on their own 30, out of time-outs, with only 83 seconds to play. Kilmer gives it all he has, but his passes fall incomplete. Then, on fourth down, he is sacked.

Don Shula had the monkey off his back, the Dolphins were the World Champions and they had become the first pro team in history to go undefeated through the Super Bowl! Not the Green Bay Packers of Vince Lombardi, not the Cleveland Browns of Paul Brown, not even the Chicago Bears of George Halas. No matter what the critics said, Don Shula had always been convinced that he would someday win the big one, and as his players carried him off the field he knew that he finally had. He would go on to another Super Bowl title the next year, but it is always the first one that is the sweetest.

THE BEST SUPER BOWL

Although it is called the Super Bowl, and the two teams in it are playing for the Vince Lombardi Trophy, symbolic of winning the championship of the National Football League, very seldom have the games really been super. But in 1979, there was a Super Bowl that will rank as one of the best football games ever played anywhere.

This was a game that had everything. It had the Dallas Cowboys, defending NFL champions, winners of 1978's Super Bowl XII. Their opponents were the Pittsburgh Steelers, who had won two Super Bowls in a row in 1975 and 1976. Their 1976 victory had been over the Cowboys, in what was, up to then,the most exciting of the Super Bowls.

Leading the Cowboys in 1979 was Roger Staubach, who had come to the Cowboys after five years on active duty with the Navy. Although only a backup quarterback when he first came to the Cowboys, Staubach soon took over the team and was the heart of its offense. With him in the backfield was Tony Dorsett, a Heisman Trophy winner for whom the Cowboys had traded top draft rights to Seattle. For the Steelers it was Terry Bradshaw. He had quarterbacked the Steelers to their first two Super Bowl wins and controlled an offense that featured a very balanced attack, with Rocky Bleier and Franco Harris leading the running attack, and Lynn Swann and John Stallworth serving as Bradshaw's great receivers. Both teams featured All Pro performers on the defense, with Mean Joe Greene and Jack Lambert leading the Steelers, and Randy Wright and Ed 'Too Small' Jones leading the Cowboys. When the two weeks of hoopla ended, and the teams met on the turf of the Orange Bowl,

ABOVE: *Super Bowl XIII: Steeler QB Terry Bradshaw (12) fades back to pass.*

LEFT: *Dallas QB Roger Staubach (12). In this game he passed for 228 and three TDs. Bradshaw passed for 318 and four TDs.*

millions felt that they would see a game worthy of the name of the man on the title trophy.

Both teams' defenses had nicknames. The Cowboys' were still the 'Doomsday Defense' and the Steelers' were called the 'Steel Curtain.' On this day both might as well have been called the 'Swiss Cheese'. Bradshaw and the Steelers got on the board early after they recovered a Cowboys fumble on their 47. Bradshaw quickly went deep and, after a couple of completions, finished the drive with a 28-yard pass to John Stallworth for the touchdown. Three Dallas defenders had gone over to cover Swann, and Bradshaw easily hit Stallworth for the first score.

Dallas gets its first break when Too Tall Jones recovers a Bradshaw fumble after Harvey Martin hits the Steelers' quarterback. Three plays later, Staubach hits Tony Hill flying down the sidelines. He is all alone and goes for a 39-yard touchdown. After the Cowboys kick off, the Steelers move steadily down the field. On third and long the Cowboys blitz the passing Bradshaw, and Tommy Henderson knocks the ball loose from Bradshaw as he tries to shift it from one hand to the other. The loose ball is picked up by Mike Hegeman of the Cowboys, and he goes 37 yards to put the Cowboys ahead 14-7.

Bradshaw and Stallworth get the Steelers even. On the third play, Bradshaw fades to pass and throws a quick hook pass to Stallworth. The great receiver catches the ball and quickly swings away from Aaron Kyle, the lone Cowboy defender covering Stallworth. The pass has gone 10 yards, and now Stallworth takes it the remaining 65 for a touchdown.

With the score tied, the Steel Curtain suddenly drops on the Cowboys, and they seem unable to make any more headway. Late in the second quarter Staubach tries a pass to get them going, but Mel Blount, the Steelers' cornerback, steps in front of the Dallas receiver, and the Steelers have the ball on their 44-yard line. But there are just seconds left. Bradshaw begins to attack the Cowboys with down-and-out patterns and hits Swann with two passes, to bring the ball to the Cowboys' 16. To reduce the pressure of the Cowboys' hard pass rush, Bradshaw sends Franco Harris up the gut with a draw play. Harris gets to the Cowboys' nine, and there are 26 seconds left on the clock.

After a time-out Bradshaw drops back to pass. The Cowboys pressure

LEFT: *Steeler John Stallworth (82) being congratulated after making Pittsburgh's second TD. He caught a 10-yard Bradshaw pass and ran it 65 yards.*

him, and he rolls to the right, spots Rocky Bleier in the end zone and lofts a pass over the outstretched hands of the Cowboys' linebacker. Bleier jumps and makes a great catch right inside the end line for the score. So the Steelers go into their locker room with a 21-14 lead.

In the third quarter, behind Staubach's passing and scrambling, the Cowboys get to the Steelers' 10. Coach Tom Landry sends in back-up tight end Jackie Smith with a play. Smith was one of the best tight ends in the NFL when he was with the St Louis Cardinals, but now he is just playing out the string and is delighted finally to be in a title game. The play is a swing pass to Dorsett, but as Staubach drops back to pass, he sees that the Steelers' defense has Dorsett covered. He looks for his second receiver, but he, too, is covered. But Jackie Smith is all alone in the end zone. Staubach spots him and throws an easy pass to the big end. The

LEFT: *In the third period Dallas missed a big chance when a Staubach pass to Jackie Smith, all alone in the end zone, failed.*

BELOW: *Steeler Franco Harris (32) breaks free. At the game's end Harris was the Super Bowl's leading rusher: 308 yards in three games. In 1980 it would be 354 yards.*

LEFT: *Lynn Swann was, with Stallworth, one of Bradshaw's great receivers. He made the last Steeler TD on a Bradshaw pass.*

RIGHT: *Tight end Billy Joe DuPree (89) made the first TD in the Cowboys' dramatic but unsuccessful last-minute comeback.*

ball comes in a little low, and Smith drops to his knees to make the catch. The ball hits him in the hands, and this great receiver, who has made so many fine catches, drops a sure touchdown. To salvage something, Landry takes a fieldgoal, and the Cowboys trail by four, instead of being tied.

The fourth quarter begins, and fans in the Orange Bowl and across the nation are thoroughly enjoying the play by these two fine teams. But within the space of 19 seconds the winner is apparently decided. With 10 minutes to play, on second and five, Bradshaw is pressured by the Cowboys' defenses, and as he rolls to the right with Cowboys all over him, he throws up a dying quail. The ball flutters downfield, and though both Lynn Swann and Benny Barnes of the Steelers go for the pass, it falls incomplete on the Cowboys' 23-yard line. But it is *not* third and five. After the ball falls, from far away a yellow flag comes flying towards the spot where Barnes and Swann fell. Pass Interference!

The Cowboys are livid. The official who called the interference was almost 20 yards away from the contact, while the official close to the two players didn't call anything. But the call stands, and, given new life, Bradshaw calls a trap. Franco Harris, whom the Cowboys have stopped most the the game, bursts up the middle, and the big fullback scores from 22 yards out. The Steelers, after the extra point, now lead 28-17.

The Cowboys line up to receive the Steelers' kickoff. On the front line of their blockers is the defensive star of the Doomsday Defense, Randy Wright. Like most defensive linemen, he has his hands heavily taped. The Steelers' kicker, Roy Gerela, instructed to kick deep, almost misses the ball, and it bounces downfield short of the Dallas receivers but into the taped hands of Randy Wright. As he tries to grab the ball, Wright is hit by the Steelers, and the ball pops loose. The Steelers recover on the Cowboys 18-yard line. Two plays later Bradshaw hits Swann, who makes a leaping catch in the end zone, and the game is over, Steelers-35, Cowboys-17.

But the Cowboys don't know that. The next time he gets the ball, Roger Staubach takes the Cowboys, passing and running, 89 yards down the field. On a third and 11, Staubach scrambles 18 yards to keep the drive going and then hits tight end Billy Joe DuPree with a seven-yard TD pass. There are 2:27 minutes left in the game after the extra point, and the score is Steelers-35, Cowboys-24. The ancient old ball park called the Orange Bowl is in an uproar as the fans stand and shout their approval for both teams.

Everyone knows that the Cowboys will try an onside kick, and the Steelers put up all their best receivers, backs and ends, to handle it. But no matter, the Cowboys recover when the Steelers bobble the kick. Now Staubach can't be stopped. The Steelers' defense is desperate, and they throw blitzes and double coverage at him, but he completes five of seven passes, the last to Butch Johnson and the Cowboys score with just 22 seconds to play. Pittsburgh's lead is now just four points.

This time the Cowboys' onside kick is covered by Rocky Bleier of the Steelers, and time runs out. So the men from the Iron City have won their third National Football League championship in five years. Upstairs, Art Rooney puts away the rosary beads he has been rubbing all through the game, looks upward at the overcast clouds, bows his head and says a silent prayer of thanksgiving.

The Steelers and Cowboys may not have played a perfect game, but they certainly have played the most exciting of the Super Bowls. Given such courageous play by both sides, it is unfortunate that a mistake by one of the officials may have altered the game's outcome. Months later, Pete Rozelle admitted that the official had erred on the interference call. But, then, who is to say that Bradshaw and Swann would not have been successful, even if the interference call had not been made? Either way, the gallant Dallas Cowboys, who had come so close to winning their third title, had nothing to be ashamed of.

THE CHARGERS v THE DOLPHINS in the 1982 AFC Semi-Final

Ever since their founding in the old American Football League, the Los Angeles Chargers had been a high-scoring passing team. But when they couldn't get fans in Los Angeles to attend, the Chargers had moved 90 miles down the Pacific coast to the beautiful city of San Diego. As the San Diego Chargers, under the coaching genius of Sid Gillman, the Chargers continued to be a high-scoring team. They had won the AFL championship in their second year but had never again won the brass ring. After Sid Gillman departed the Chargers and the two leagues merged, the Chargers continued to be entertaining, but their defense was never good enough to get them to the NFL title game.

After they had won back-to-back titles in 1973 and 1974, the Miami Dolphins continued to be one of pro football's best franchises, but they had not returned to the Super Bowl since then. So when they met the San Diego Chargers on 2 January 1982 in the AFC semifinals, the Dolphins knew that their defense would have to stop the deadly passing attack of Dan Fouts if they were to make it back to the glory days of the early 70s.

LEFT: *Millions of TV viewers stayed up late to watch the dramatic AFC playoff game between Miami and San Diego played on 2 January 1982 in Miami's Orange Bowl.*

To accommodate television, the two teams played at night. By the time this game ended millions of TV viewers would have stayed up long past midnight watching a game that, for sheer drama and human emotion, probably hadn't been equalled in pro football since the Packers-Cowboys championship 'Ice Bowl' game.

The Chargers took the opening kickoff and marched downfield to score on a field goal. Their much-maligned defense held the Dolphins, and Dolphins' punt was returned 56 yards by Wes

ABOVE: *Miami's Tony Nathan (22) carrying. Going into the game he was rated only average.*

LEFT: *Charger running back Chuck Muncie (46), strong, agile and a good receiver, exemplified San Diego's powerful offense.*

Chandler for another touchdown: 10-0. The Chargers' kickoff was bouncing between Dolphin players, so one of the Chargers alertly fell on it. After a few more plays Chuck Muncie scored, and it was 17-0.

The young Dolphins quarterback, David Woodley, whom Don Shula had hoped could lead the Dolphins' running attack and keep the ball away from the Chargers, tried a pass. What happened was just what Shula had feared. The Chargers picked off Woodley's pass, and four plays later Fouts hit one of his running backs, James Brooks, coming out of the backfield, and the Chargers had another touchdown. The score was 24-0, the first quarter still had time in it and the Dolphins had run only seven plays!

Shula goes to his backup quarterback, Don Strock. This tall, quiet young man had played the role of relief passer for Bob Griese and now does the same for David Woodley. At this moment his unenviable job is to rally a thoroughly bewildered team trailing by 24 points and somehow to outwit a defense that

LEFT: *Miami QB Don Strock (10) is about to throw to Duriel Harris, who will lateral to Tony Nathan for Miami's second TD.*

ABOVE RIGHT: *Dolphin QB David Woodley (16) was replaced by Strock after the Chargers piled up a 24-0 lead.*

BELOW RIGHT: *San Diego was supposed to have the offense and Miami the defense, but both did well in both categories.*

knows he'll have to pass to get back in the game.

In the second period Strock takes the Dolphins downfield, and they come away with a fieldgoal: At least they have scored. Now all that is needed is for their defense to wake up and stop Fouts and the Chargers. They do, and the next time Strock gets the ball, the Dolphins again march downfield, and Strock passes to his tight end, Joe Rose, for a touchdown. It is now 24-10, with the clock winding down. When the Dolphins force the Chargers to punt, they get the ball on the Chargers' 40. But there are only six seconds left. Now Shula and Strock come up with a play that has been part of playground touch football since kids started playing the game. Call it anything you want – 'the hook and go,' or 'the pass and lateral' – but that's what these professionals fall back on. Strock passes over the middle to Harris, and as the Chargers fall on him, he flips the ball to Tony Nathan, streaking by. The Chargers are too stunned to do anything. Nathan is so alone he just trots into the end zone, and the huge Miami throng in the Orange Bowl goes crazy. As the gun ends the first half, the Chargers' seemingly insurmountable lead is now down to 24-17. And as Al Jolson said in *The Jazz Singer*, 'You ain't heard nothing yet.'

In the second half the Dolphins take the opening kickoff, immediately carve out huge chunks of yardage on Strock's passing and tie the game, 24-24, when Ross takes a pass over the middle and scores from 15 yards out.

The rap on the Chargers has always been that they can score big but they can't stop anyone. A more insidious comment by some experts is that they are front runners and lack the guts to come back against a good team in a critical situation. Now it is Dan Fouts's turn to prove those experts wrong. Fouts takes the Chargers right back down the field and hits his great tight-end, Kellen Winslow, with a 25-yard touchdown pass. Chargers-31, Dolphins-24.

But Strock retaliates, tying the score with a 50-yard touchdown pass to Bruce Hardy. Then, on the first play of the fourth quarter, Tony Nathan rips through the Chargers' defense for a 12-yard run, and the Dolphins are back on top. 38-31. The Dolphins contain the Chargers on the next round, and now Strock begins a long ball-control drive designed both to eat up the clock and to keep the ball away from Dan Fouts. There were a little over 11 minutes left in the game when the Dolphins began the drive. There are just 4:28 minutes left in the game when the drive ends.

But it doesn't end as Shula had hoped. Rookie fullback Andra Franklin takes Strock's handoff at the Chargers' 21-yard line and cracks into the middle. Struggling for extra yardage, he lets the ball get away from his body, and when he is slammed by defensive tackle Gary Johnson, linebacker Linden King grabs the ball loose from the rookie. The ball falls to the turf, and the Chargers' Pete Shaw covers it.

For someone like Dan Fouts, four minutes to go is a lifetime. Shula and the Dolphins know that, and it is up to their defense to stop Fouts. Easier said than done. In 10 plays Fouts has his team on the Dolphins' nine-yard line.

BETTERS

PRESTON
29

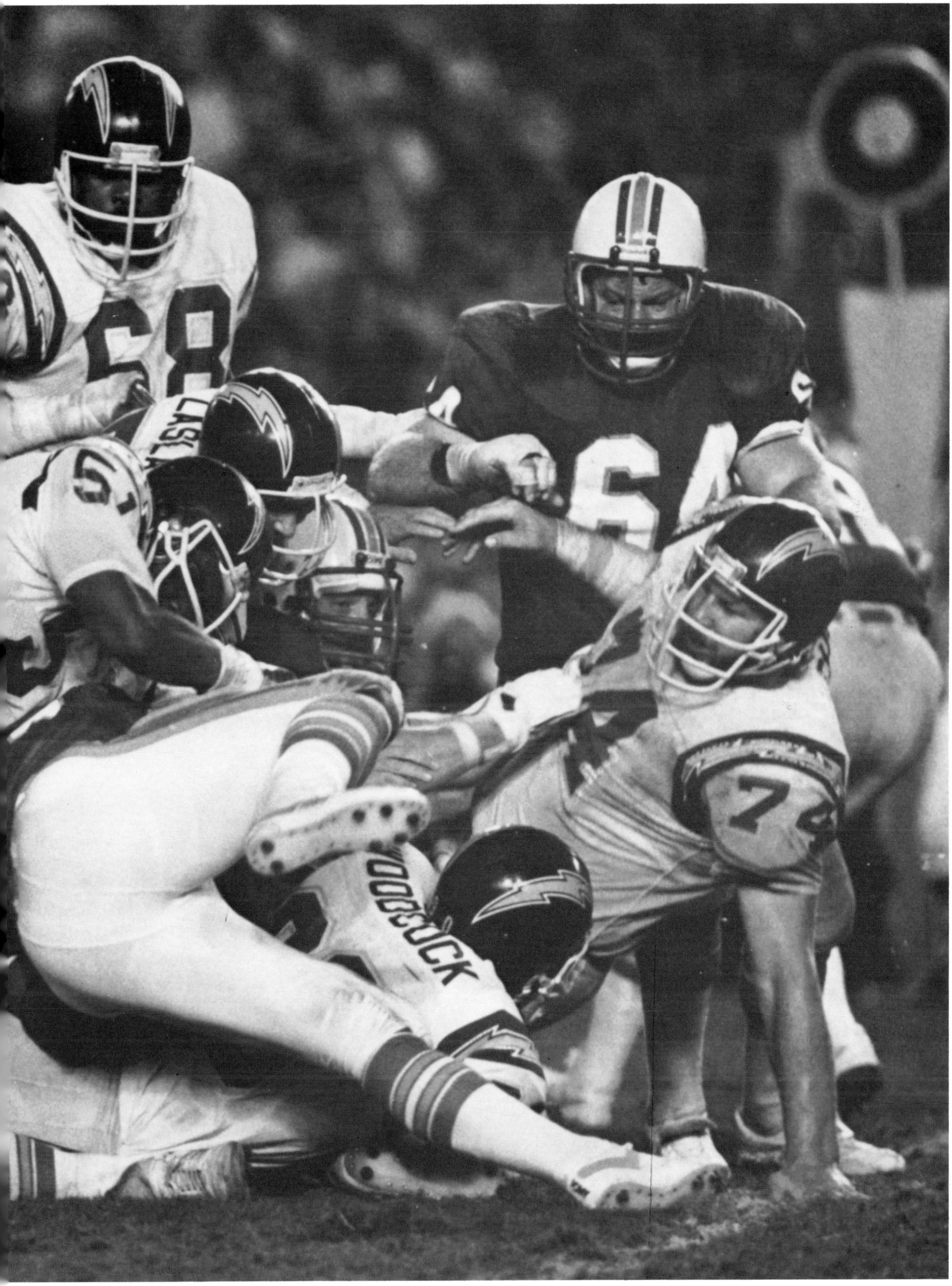
68
64
74
WOODCOCK

PREVIOUS PAGE: *In the fourth period Dolphin fullback Andra Franklin is hit by a mob of Charger defenders. His fumble was recovered by San Diego's Pete Shaw.*

ABOVE: *Ace Charger QB Dan Fouts prepares to pass. In the game he completed 33 of 53 passes for 433 yards and three TDs.*

RIGHT: *San Diego kicker Rolf Benirschke. He kicked the Chargers' first three points, and the winning three in overtime.*

With the crowd pleading for the defense to stop him, Fouts sends Winslow into the end zone, where half the Dolphins are waiting for him. Fouts turns from Winslow, spots Jim Brooks trailing and hits him with the touchdown pass. The extra point is good, and the teams are tied.

There are still 58 seconds to play, and in this game, and with these teams, that is more than enough time to win. But Miami's chances seem to go down the drain when a Strock pass is intercepted by Willie Buchanan. But as he tries to get up field, he is hit, fumbles and the Dolphins recover! Strock immediately hits Nathan for 17 yards, and Tommy Vigorito picks up six more on a run. The ball is on the Chargers' 25, and Shula goes for a fieldgoal.

Uwe von Schamann, the Dolphins' excellent kicker, comes in for an

RIGHT: *San Diego's Charlie Joiner caught three of Fouts's passes in a row to bring Benirschke in range of the final fieldgoal.*

BELOW: *Dolphins' kicker Uwe von Schamann (5) and Bruce Hardy. Von Schamann kicked one-for-three.*

attempt from 42 yards away, well within his range.The Chargers know they need to block the kick, so they include Kellen Winslow in the reception committee in the hope that his height and leaping ability will help them block the kick. The Dolphins line up and, with the snap, both lines collide and von Schamann hits the ball hard and straight. But it never gets past the line of scrimmage, for Winslow leaps up and swats the ball off course. Overtime.

Fouts now takes the Chargers quickly downfield, and with the ball on the Dolphins' nine-yard line, Don Coryell, the Chargers' coach, sends in kicker Rolfe Benirschke to win the game. But he misses the chip shot from 26 yards out, and the ball goes over to Miami. There are a little over six minutes left in the overtime.

Several times in this game, Kellen Winslow, after catching a pass and making a long run, had not gotten up after he was tackled. He would be hauled off to the sidelines, and Miami fans always hoped that was the last they would see of him. But the Chargers' trainers would work furiously on the wounded warrior, and the next time the Chargers had the ball, there would be the amazing Winslow. Now, in this overtime period, everyone on the field felt the way the battered Winslow looked. Both teams were exhausted and playing on sheer adrenaline and nerves.

With his last reserves of strength Strock rallies the Dolphins and brings them back downfield, the big play being a 21-yard pass to Jimmy Cefalo. Three running plays bring the ball dead center in the field on the Chargers' 25-yard line. In comes von Schamann, and the teams line up to end this exciting, draining game. But again the Chargers rise to the challenge, and it is defensive end Leroy Jones who is San Diego's new hero, blocking von Schamann's kick.

San Diego's ball, with less than six minutes to go. Everyone, in the stands, watching on television and listening to the game on the radio is exhausted. And they haven't even been getting hit. Many hope the game will be called because there should be no loser in this great contest.

But Dan Fouts isn't interested in a tie. The Dolphins' defenders have been beating on his bones all night. They have pressured him on almost every pass, and even after he throws the ball they still slam him to the ground. Now he means to show something to all those self-appointed experts who said that the Chargers couldn't win the big game. Two passes to Chandler pick up 27 yards, and after each pass Fouts has to drag himself up off the turf.

The Chargers are on the Miami 49 when Fouts again goes back to pass. This time he finds Charlie Joiner deep over the middle and fires a strike. The play ends on the Dolphins' nine-yard line, and now the Chargers go for the fieldgoal. This time Benirschke knocks it right through the uprights, and at last the Chargers are on their way to the AFC title game.

For nearly four hours these two fine teams had moved up and down the field with an offensive display never matched in a playoff game. The players on both sides proved repeatedly that no lead was too big to overcome, no sacrifice too great to make for victory. The fact that the Chargers ultimately won was of secondary importance, for the way this game was played completely overshadowed its outcome. And as every bleary-eyed fan of either team realized, this is what football is finally all about.

MICHIGAN
M
ATHLETIC MEDICINE
Dr. Sandall
HONDA
91
55
48

MICHIGAN v OHIO STATE 1986

There are many great rivalries in intercollegiate football, and over the years all of them have contributed memorable episodes to the lore of the college game. The oldest continuing rivalry is Harvard and Yale. They have been having at each other since 1883, and while nowadays the outcome doesn't effect the selection of who wins the mythical national championship, the tradition and color of that annual bash provides the Ivy League with its only assured sellout each season.

There is also the Stanford-University of California match in the San Francisco Bay area: Out there they call it 'The Big Game.' And then there is Nebraska v Oklahoma. Often their last game decides the Big Eight titleholder. The biggest non-conference rivalry, and one that sometimes does decide who the national champion will be is that between Notre Dame and Southern California. And there are other famous regional rivalries – Alabama and Auburn, Texas and Texas A & M, Georgia and Georgia Tech and many more.

But year in and out, the rivalry that probably generates the most excitement nationwide is the annual final game of the Big Ten season played between the Wolverines of the University of Michigan and the Buckeyes of Ohio State. Since 1944, when the schedule-makers in the Big Ten decided that the two schools would always meet in their last game of the season, the Big Ten title has been decided 18 times.

Probably the most memorable of these famous matches was the famous 'Snow Bowl' game played in 1950 at Columbus. A blizzard had swept across the Midwest and had closed roads throughout the area from Chicago to Pittsburgh. The visiting Michigan team didn't get to Columbus until late Friday night. The huge horseshoe

LEFT: *The Michigan Wolverines leave the field at halftime in the 1986 edition of the annual Michigan-Ohio classic.*

that is the Buckeyes' stadium was covered with three feet of snow. Radio stations all over Ohio warned fans to stay home. But they might as well have saved their breath.

After all, this game was for the Big Ten title, and it was the Michigan game. The Ohio State Athletic Director and his counterpart at Michigan had considered cancelling the game, but when they saw the thousands who were coming to the game, trudging through the bitter cold and high winds, they decided that they had to play.

Throughout the game the snow came down so hard that most of the fans in the stands had no idea of what was happening. The public address announcer had to leave the warmth of the press box and go down on the sidelines to give the play-by-play for the fans. Late in the game, Michigan's defense was holding Ohio State deep in Ohio territory. Vic Janowicz, the future Heisman trophy winner, went back to punt the ball out of the end zone. But the Wolverines rushed him, blocked the punt and recovered in the end zone for the only touchdown in game. They won, 9-6, won the Big Ten title and went on to win the Rose Bowl.

In the 70s Archie Griffin of Ohio State became the only player to ever win the Heisman Trophy twice, and he did it by leading the Buckeyes to wins over Michigan. In 1977 Michigan defeated the Buckeyes at Ann Arbor before the largest crowd in college football history. Over 106,000 fans watched Michigan stop a late Ohio State drive deep in Wolverine territory when Michigan recovered a Buckeye fumble. Ohio State's volatile coach, Woody Hayes, became so incensed that he punched out a television camera and cameraman on the sidelines.

ABOVE: *In 1986 the lynchpin of the Michigan offense was QB Jim Harbaugh (4), here with tackle Mike Husar (74).*

LEFT: *One of the most famous Michigan-OSU duels was the 'Snow Bowl' game, fought in 1950 in a blinding snowstorm.*

Completely typical of the many great games that have been played in this legendary series was the one that took place on 22 November 1986. Going into the season, both teams were considered contenders for the national title, but Ohio State lost its first two non-conference games, killing any chance for being Number One at the end of the season. But the Buckeyes nevertheless won their next nine games and went into the Michigan game in first place in the Big Ten.

Meanwhile, Michigan had been roll-

ABOVE: *Ohio's excellent QB Jim Karsatos (16) being rushed by Billy Harris (56).*

RIGHT: *Ohio's Chris Carter (2) receiving.*

ing along undefeated and was seriously in contention for the national honors until the week before the Ohio State clash. That week they entertained Minnesota, a team they had defeated so many times over the past two decades that the trophy they played for, the Little Brown Jug, hadn't been out of the trophy room in Ann Arbor for years. But in the Big Ten you can never take any opponent lightly, and Minnesota upset Michigan with a dramatic fieldgoal in the final seconds. Gone was the shot at a national title, and now the Wolverines headed for Columbus knowing they must win to tie for the Big Ten title and have a chance to go to the Rose Bowl.

Even though there is always plenty of excitement before a Michigan-Ohio State game, Jim Harbaugh, Michigan's fine quarterback, now decided that it was time to add a little more. So early in the week he told a few reporters covering the Wolverines' practice that he, Jim Harbaugh, 'will guarantee that we'll beat Ohio State.' Shades of Joe Namath. The ink was barely dry on the Columbus newspapers before Harbaugh's quote was posted on every

ABOVE: *Karsatos calls the play in an OSU huddle. Ohio dominated the first half, and Michigan the second.*

LEFT: *Michigan's Monte Robbins (43) holds for Mike Gillette (19).*

RIGHT: *Michigan running back Jamie Morris (23), assisted by the blocking of Mike Dames and Mike Hammerstein, races through a hole.*

bulletin board in Ohio State. Ohio's coaching staff were delighted, and the Michigan coaches couldn't believe it. Ohio State was tough enough without giving them extra incentive.

When the day of the great game arrived more than 97,000 roaring fans jammed the stadium at Columbus. The crowds at these games almost never stop cheering, and when Jamie Holland returned the Wolverines' opening kickoff into Michigan territory, the old stadium rocked so much that the television announcers could feel the movement high atop the field.

This edition of the Buckeyes was a passing team, and quarterback Jim Karsatos immediately hit running back Vince Workman for a deep penetration into Michigan territory. Another run by Workman and a pass to their great wide receiver, Chris Carter, and the Buckeyes were on the Michigan four. Karsatos then quickly lofted a touch pass to Carter, who had one-on-one coverage, and Ohio State scored.

The Wolverines quickly drove back into Buckeye territory, but the Ohio State defense held them firmly enough to make them settle for a fieldgoal. The Buckeyes then took the next kickoff and marched straight down the field on Karsatos's passing. With first and 10, he pitched out to Workman, who left a string of Michigan defenders in his wake as he went 46 yards into the Michigan end zone.

Again the Wolverines drove down field, and again Ohio State stopped them short. They got a fieldgoal in the second quarter, but at the half, it was Ohio State leading 14-6 and heading for another Big Ten crown. The Buckeyes had run around and through the vaunted Michigan defense, and Karsatos had been able to pass the Buckeyes up and down the field.

In the third quarter, however, the Michigan defense gears up and begins to pressure Karsatos and to stop the Buckeyes' running game. Although Harbaugh had moved the Wolverines

ABOVE: *Buckeye running back Vince Workman. Workman scored Ohio's second TD by running a pass 46 yards.*

RIGHT: *Michigan's coach, Bo Schembechler (right) was outraged when officials failed to call a pass interference on a linebacker who decked Harbaugh.*

in the first half, he hadn't been able to get them in the end zone. Now, Harbaugh gets the Wolverines going with short passes and by handing the ball off to diminutive Jamie Morris, his fine running back. Between them they at last manage to get within striking distance of the Ohio goal, and Morris scores on a four-yard run. The score is now Ohio State-14, Michigan-13. The Buckeyes immediately retaliate, driving back up the field and getting a fieldgoal to raise the bet 17-13.

Michigan answers with Morris's runs and Harbaugh's passing, but a receiver drops a sure touchdown, and Michigan punts. Ohio State can't mount anything, and they are also forced to punt. In the Woody Hayes days, the Ohio defense had kept the scores down. Michigan coach Bo Schembechler, an assistant under Hayes before going to Michigan, also believes in ball control, but for the first time in his career at Michigan, his team has gained more yardage passing than

running.

Again Harbaugh brings Michigan downfield, and Jamie Morris makes a big play when he breaks a tackle at the line of scrimmage and, behind great downfield blocking, scoots 52 yards to the Ohio State 17. A few plays later, he breaks off tackle and scores from the eight. For the first time Michigan is ahead, 19-17.

Schembechler wants to make it necessary for Ohio State to score a touchdown to beat him, so he orders Harbaugh to go for the two-point conversion. As Harbaugh drops back to pass, the Ohio State defenders cover his receivers, so he looks for his safety valve, the fullback circling out of the backfield. But as Harbaugh throws the ball the fullback is decked by an Ohio State linebacker. This is clearly pass interference, and Michigan will have the ball on the Ohio State one. But the officials don't throw the yellow flag and rule the conversion incomplete.

Bo Schembechler, who had had a heart attack a few seasons back, is almost apoplectic. He runs out onto the field and points to the spot where his player was knocked down. He storms up and down the sidelines, and finally the officials throw the flag . . . penalizing the Michigan bench 15 yards.

Nevertheless, as the teams go into the fourth quarter the Michigan defense seems to have taken the play away from the Buckeyes. On his next possession Harbaugh again brings Michigan deep into Buckeye territory, until a fumble stops the drive. But the Buckeyes can't move and are forced to punt. There are 10 minutes left when Michigan gets the ball. This time they don't fumble or drop sure touchdowns. Morris's running and Harbaugh's passing get them to Ohio State's eight. When Thomas Wilcher, the young man who fumbled earlier, scores, the Wolverines lead by nine points and it looks like they are headed for Pasadena.

But the Buckeyes are made of stern stuff, and Jim Karsatos brings them back. With thousands cheering them on, the Buckeyes charge downfield, and when Karsatos hits Carter in the end zone with a 17-yard scoring pass, the Buckeyes are only two down after the extra point is made by freshman kicker Matt Frantz. The Buckeyes then get the break they need when Wilcher fumbles again, deep in Buckeye territory. There are 3:17 minutes left, plenty of time to get within fieldgoal range.

Karsatos's passing brings the Buckeyes downfield, but as they move into

BELOW: *Harbaugh gets off a pass. He had earlier 'guaranteed' a Michigan victory.*

Michigan territory the Wolverines stiffen. There are a few seconds left, and it is fourth and one on the Michigan 25. If the Buckeyes go for the first down and make it, they can get closer for the winning fieldgoal. But if Michigan stops them, it is all over. Coach Earl Bruce decides that his Buckeyes will go to Pasadena on the leg of his freshman kicker. It will be a 42-yard attempt – difficult, but within Frantz's range.

The teams line up, with some of the Michigan defenders jumping up and down trying to shake up the freshman. With the snap of the ball, the lines collide, and the Michigan defenders frantically try to get through the blockers. The ball is in place, and Frantz jogs forward from his kicking position. His shoe slams into the ball, and it takes off for the goal posts. The young men on the field all watch as the ball begins to move away from the uprights and pass them, wide to the left!

So it is all over: Michigan-26 and Ohio-24. The television cameras capture the excitement and happiness of the Michigan players. Then one camera flashes the picture of a freshman with tears in his eyes, his teammates trying to console him. Young Matt Frantz will have three more years to get even with Michigan, and if the past is prologue, he probably will.

Thus this storied rivalry added another chapter to an already golden history. As the years pass, the names of the players and coaches in both schools will change many times, but the old feeling will remain. And because of that we can take it as given that the Michigan-Ohio State games of the future will continue to represent everything that is most admirable and most attractive in American football.

BELOW: *OSU's coach Earl Bruce. Only Matt Frantz's missed fieldgoal prevented Bruce's Buckeyes from going to the Rose Bowl.*

INDEX

Adamle, Tony 60
Adderley, Herb 86, 87, 95
Albert, Frankie 44
All American Football Conference 56, 58
Allan, George 117, *120*, 120
Ameche, Alan *73*, 76, 78, *79*, 79
American Football League 79, *80*, 94, 108, 109, 113
Anderson, Don 101, *103*, 103, 105-07
Antenucci, Frank *32*
Army *49*, *50*, 52, 62, 70; Columbia *52*, 52-5; Navy *11*, 48, **1950** *67*, *68*, *69* 67-9, *70*; Notre Dame 18, 48, 50, **1913** 12-13, **1946** *49*, 50

Bakke, Tom 67, *68*
Baldinger, Jim *68*, 68
Baltimore Colts 56, 72, 87, 102, 108, *109* Giants **1958** *73*, 76-9, *76*, *77*, *79*; Jets 110-12, *111*, *112*
Bannerman, Dave 67
Barrett, Billy 63
Battles, Cliff *35*, 36
Baugh, Sam *34*, 34-7, *35*, *38*, 46, 47
Beathard, Pete *91*, *92*, 92
Bell, Bert 72
Benirschke, Rolfe *132*, 133
Berry, Raymond 76, *77*, *78*, *79*
Bertelli, Angelo 49, 63
Big Ten 20, 31, 62, 90-1, 135
Blaik, Bob 67, 68, 69, *70*
Blaik, Earl 49, 67, *70*, 70
Blanchard, Doc *49*, *50*, 50
Bleier, Rocky 121, 123, 134
Blood, Johnny *See* McNally
Boston Redskins 34
Boucher, Frank *32*
Bowman, Ken 95, 103, 107
Bradshaw, Terry 113, *114*, 114-15, *115*, *121*, 121-4
Brenner, Fred 63
Brink, Larry 60
Brown, Paul *56*, 56, 57, *61*, 113
Brown, Larry 117, *118*
Brown, Roger 88, *89*
Brown, Rosie 86
Brown, Willie *91*, 92
Bruce, Matt *142*
Brumbaugh, Carl 29
Bryant, Goble *53*
Buffalo All Americans *17*
Buffalo Bills 97, 117
Bumgardner, Rex 61
Buoniconti, Nick *120*, 120
Butcher, Ron 92

California, University of, Golden Bears 62
Camp, Walter Chauncey 8, *9*
Canton Bulldogs *14*, *15*, 15-16
Carlisle Indian School *15*
Carter, Chris *137*, 139, 141
Chabot, Ed *49*
Chandler, Don 77, 78, 94, 98, 107
Chandler, Wes 127, 133
Chicago Bears *7*, 10, *23*, 23-4, *25*, 28, 35, *45*, 50, 59, 72, 83, 87, 102; Giants **1925** *24*, 24-5, **1933** 28, **1934** 29-30; Redskins 36-7, **1940** *44*, 44-7, *46*
Chicago Cardinals 24, 59, 72
Chicago, University of 4
Chirra, Charles 69
Clarke, Fred 95-6
Cleveland Browns 56, 57-8, 72, 76, 94, 102, 110, 117; Rams **1950** 59-61, *60*, *61*
Cleveland Rams 56
Colorado, University of 52
Columbia University Lions: Army defeat *52*, 52-5, *53*, *54*, *55*
Conerly, Charles 72, *73*, 76, *77*, *77*, 78, 86
Cotton Bowl 63, *95*, 95, *96*

Crisler, Herbert 62
Csonka, Larry *116*, 117
Crow, Lindon 78
Crowley, Jim *19*, 19, *41*, 41, 62

Dale, Carroll 98, 99
Dallas Cowboys *4*, *7*, 10, 116; Packers **1967** *94*, *95*, *96*, 95-6, NFL title game *103*, *104*, 103-07; Steelers 121-24, *121*, *123*, *124*
Daly, Charley 13
Danielson, Gary 66
Danowski, Ed *28*, 29, 30
Davis, Glenn *49*, *50*, 50, 60
Davis, Willie *84*, 84, 95, 104
Dawson, Len 66, *97*, 97, 98-9, *99*, 101
Detroit Lions 72, 102; Packers **1962** 87-8, and 'Massacre' 88-9, *89*
'Doomsday Defense' 95, 103, 104
Dorais, Charles 12, *13*, 13
Dorsett, Tony 121
Dowler, Boyd 84, 95, 98, 103, *104*, 105
Druze, John *41*, *42*
Dupre, L G 78
Dupree, Billy Joe *124*, 124

Eastern Conference 59; title 72, 76, 95
Edwards, Turk 37
Ellis, William Webb 7
Ewbank, Weeb *110*, 110, 111

Fears, Tom 59
Fischer, Pat 119, 120
flying wedge formation 8, *9*
Foldberg, Dan 67, *68*, 69
Fordham Rams *1*, *40*, 40, 41-3, 41*n*, *42*
The Four Horsemen *19*, 19
Fouts, Dan 127, 128, 132, *132*, 133
Frankiun, Ike 29
Franklin, Andra 128, *132*
Frantz, Matt 141, 142
Fuqua, John 114, *115*

Gaiters, Bobbyy 86
Galifa, Arnold 52, 54, *54*, 55
Garrett, Mike 97, 101
Gatski, Frank 61
Gerela, Roy 113, 124
Gibson, Billy 24
Gifford, Frank 72, 76, 77, 86
Gillman, Sid 127
Gillom, Horace 57, 60
Gipp, George 14, 48-9, *49*
Goldberg, Marshall *40*, 41, 42
Grabowski, Jim 95, 101, 103
Graham, Otto *57*, 57, 58, 59, *60*, 60, 61
Grange, Red 10, 18, 20-2, *21*, *22*, *23*, 23, *24*, 24, *25*, 25, 28
Great Lakes Naval Training Center Bluejackets 56, 63
Green Bay Packers 10, 34, 41, 80-1, 88, 108; Chiefs *97*, *99*, 97-101, *101*; Colts **1965** 94; Cowboys **1967** *94*, *95*, *96*, 95-6, for 3rd NFL title *103*, *104*, *107*, 108-07; Giants **1961** *84*, 84-6; Lions **1962** 87-8, Thanksgiving 'Massacre 88-9, *89*; Lombardi's molding of 81-3; rivalries 87
Greene, Joe *113*, 113, 121
Gregg, Forrest 81, 86, 103, 107
Gremminger, Hank 84, 86
Grier, Roosevelt *73*, 76
Griese, Bob 66, 117, *118*, 119, 120
Griffin, Archie 136
Groza, Lou *56*, 57, 60, *61*, 61
Gurski, John 69
Gushurst, Fred 12
Gustafson, Bill *54*

Halas, George *23*, 23, 24, *25*, *28*, 28, 44, 46, 56, 81
Hall of Fame 56*n*, 57, 72, 86
Harbaugh, Jim *136*, 137, 140, *141*, 141

Harper, Jess 12, 13
Harris, Franco 113, 114-15, *115*, 121, 122, *123*, 124
Hart, Gerald *69*
Hart, Leon 63, 72
Harvard University 8, 18
Hauff, Frank 67
Hayes, Bob 95
Heffelfinger, William 14, *15*
Hein, Mel 30
Heisman Trophy *49*, 49, 50, 72, 82
Herber, Arnie 35, 81, *81*
Hill, Fred 92
Hill, Jerry 111, 112
Hirsh, Elroy 59
Horner, Bob 59, 60
Hornung, Paul 82, *83*, 83, *84*, 84, *86*, 86, 87, 98, 102, 103
Howell, Jim Lee 77, 81
Huff, Sam 72, *76*, 76, *79*, 84, 86
Hunt, Lamar *94*, 94, 101
Hutson, Don 81

'Ice Bowl' 103-07
Illinois, University of 18, 19, 52, 90, 91; Michigan **1923** 20-2, **1924** *21*
Irwin, Don 37

James, Tommy 60, 61
Jones, Biff 70
Jones, Ed 121, 122
Jones, Edgar 'Dub' 56, 58, 60
Jones, Gomer 31
Jones, Leroy 133
Jouett, John 12
Jurgensen, Sonny 117
Justice, Ed 37

Kansas City Chiefs/Packers *97*, *99*, 97-101, *101*
Karilivacz, Carl *76*, *79*
Karras, Alex *87*, 87, 88, *89*
Karsatos, Jim *137*, *139*, 139, 141-42
Katcavage, Jim 77
Kellett, Don 72
Kiick, Jim 117, 120
Kilmer, Billy 117, *118*, 120
King, Phil 77
Kramer, Jerry 103, 106, 107
Kramer, Ron 84, 86, 99
Kroner, Gary 92
Kusserow, Lou 52, *53*, *54*, 54
Kyle, Aaron 122

Lambeau, Earl 80
Lamonica, Daryle 109, 113
Landry, Tom 104, 123-24
Lavelli, Dante 57, 58, 59, 60
Layden, Elmer *19*, 19, *31*, 31
Layne, Bobby 72
leagues 8, 56, 79, 127; divisions 28, 59, and conferences 102; franchises 10, 26, 56, 80
Leahy, Frank 47, 49, *50*, 62-3, 65, *66*, 66
Lilly, Bob *94*, 95, 106-07
Livingston, Cliff 76
Lombardi, Vince 19, 41, *42*, 70, 76, 77, 86, 88, 117; as Packers' coach 80, *81*, 81-4, *86*, 86, 88, 98, 99, 102-03, 104, 105, 107, *107*, 108; trophy 121
Los Angeles Chargers 127
Los Angeles Rams 56, 59, 117; Browns **1950** 59-61, *60*, *61*
Luckman, Sid 45, *45*, 45, 46
Lujack, Johnny *50*, 59

Maccioli, Mike 65
McAfee, George *44*, *45*, 45, *46*, 46
McBride, Mickey 56, *61*
McElhenny, Hugh 72
McGee, Max 95, 98
McGill University 8
McHan, Lamar 82
McNally, John *80*, 80
McWilliams, Tom *50*
Madden, John 113
Manders, Jack 29, *36*, 36

Maniaci, Joe 46
Mara, Tim *24*, 24
Mara, Wellington 99
Marchetti, Gino 76, *77*, 77
Marshall, George Preston *26*, 26, 28, 34, 45, 81
Maryland, University of 66
Massillion Tigers *14*, 16
Masterson, Bernie *36*, 36, 37
Matson, Ollie 72
Matte, Tom 111
Mecom, John 102
Mercein, Chuck 105, 106-07
Meredith, Don 95, 96, *104*, 104
Miami Dolphins *3*, 113; Chargers **1982** 127-33, *127*, *128*, *132*, *133*; Redskins *116*, 117-20, *117*, *118*, *120*; unbeaten season 116-18
Michigan State 41, 62, 67
Michigan, University of, Wolverines 10, 18, 19, 20; Illinois **1923** 20-2; Ohio State **1986** *135*, *139*, *141*, 137-42
Miller, Don *19*, 19
Millner, Wayne 32, 36, 37
Minnesota, University of 137
Modzelewski, Dick *73*, 76, 78
Molenda, John 30
Molesworth, Keith 29
Moore, Lenny 76, 78
Morrall, Earl 110, 111, *112*, *117*
Morris, Eugene 117
Morris, Jamie *139*, 140, 141
Motley, Marion *57*, 57, 58, 59, 60
Mutscheller, Jim 79
Myhra, Steve *76*, 78, *79*

Nagurski, Bronco *26*, *28*, 28, 29, *30*, 30, 36-7
Namath, Joe 97, 108-10, *109*, 111, 112
Nathan Tony *127*, 127, 132
NFL title games 10, 28, 44, 58, 63, 66, 72, 83, 88, 94, 95, 101, 102-07, 110, 127
National Football League 9, 26, 72, 109; AAFC competition 56, 94; expansion 102; exhibition games 6, *7*; franchises 24, 34
Navy 18; Army **1950** *67*, 67-9, *68*, *70*
Neale, Earle 58
Nebraska, University of 44
Nevers, Ernie *19*, 19
New Orleans Saints 102
New York Giants 10, 17, 24, 41, 59, 72, 83, 87, 88; Bears **1925** 24-5, **1933** 28, **1934** *28*, 29-30; Colts **1958** *73*, 76-9, *76*, *77*, *79*; Packers **1961** *84*, 84-6, *86*
New York Jets 108, 117; Colts 110-12, *111*; Raiders 108-12
Nitschke, Ray *84*, 84, 95, 108
Noll, Chuck 113, 114
Nolting, Ray 36, *45*, 45
North Carolina, University of, 65
Northwestern University Wildcats 57
Notre Dame *19*, 62, *62*, 63; Army rivalry 48-9, 50, **1913** 12-13, **1924** 18, **1946** *49*, 50; Ohio State *31*, 31-2, *32*; Pittsburgh 41; Purdue *63*, *65*, 65-6, *66*; SMU **1949** 63; *See also* The Four Horsemen

Oakland Raiders 108-09; Steelers 113-15, *115*
O'Brien, Davy 40
Ohio State University Buckeyes 56, 57, 90; Michigan **1986** *137*, *139*, *140*, 137-42; Notre Dame *31*, 31-3, *32*
Oklahoma All Stars 17
Oklahoma Sooners, University of, 62
Olsen, Bill 54
Orr, Jimmy 111, 112
Osmanski, Bill *44*, *45*, 45, *46*, *47*
Owen, Steve 17

Pac Eight 90
Parilli, Vito 81
Patton, Jim *73*, *79*, *84*
Perry, Joe 72
Petibon, John 65
Philadelphia Eagles *59*, 83, 102; Cleveland Browns 58-9
Pilney, Andy 31, *32*, 32
Pinckert, Ernie *35*, 36
Piska, Joe 12
Pitt Panthers (University of Pittsburgh) *1*, *40*, 40-3, *42*
Pitts, Elijah 95, *101*, 101, 103
Pittsburgh Steelers 59, 72, 117; Cowboys *4*, 121-24; Raiders **1969** 113-15, *115*
Plum, Milt 87-8, *87*
Pollard, Vic 67
Pool, Hampton *46*
Poole, George *49*
Princeton University 8, *9*, 18
Pritchard, Vernon 12
Providence (RI) Steamrollers *26*, 26
Purdue University Boilermakers: Notre Dame **1950** *63*, *65*, 65-6
Pyle, C C *23*, 23

Rechichar, Bert 77
Reeves, Dan *95*, 95, 96, 104
Reich, Gil 67
Renfro, Mel 103, *104*
Rice, Grantland 19, 20
Richardson, Willie 110
Richter, Pat *92*, 92
Ringo, Jim 86
Robinson, Dave 96, 101
Robustelli, Andy 76, 77, 86
Rockne, Knute *12*, 12, *13*, 13, 14; as coach 18, *19*, 19, 31, 41, 48-9, 62, 65
Ronzani, Gene 30
Rooney, Art 114, 115
Rose Bowl game 10, *19*, 19, 41, 44, *90*, 90-1; **1963** game 92
Rosenbloom, Carroll 110, 116, 117
Rossides, Gene 52, *53*, 53, 54
Rote, Kyle *63*, 63, *76*, 76, *77*, 86
Rowan, Rip 52, 53, 54
Rowecamp, Bill *69*
Rugby (game) *7*, 7-8
Rutgers University 8, *9*
Rymkus, Lou 56

Sample, Johnny 111, 112
Samuels, Dale *65*, 65
San Diego Chargers: Dolphins **1982** 127-33, *127*, *128*, *132*, *133*
San Francisco 49ers 56
Sauer, George 110, 111
Schembechler, Bo *140*
Schmidt, Joe 87, 88
Schnelker, Bob 77
Seven Blocks of Granite 19, *40*, 40-3, *42*
Shakespeare, Bill *32*, 32-3
Shaughnessy, Clark 44, *45*, 47
Shofer, Del 83, *84*
Shula, Don 110, 116-17, *117*, 120, 127
single wing formation 22, 40, 44
Sitko, Emil 63
Skoronski, Bob 86, 101, 103
Smith, Billy 'Bubba' 110, *111*, 111
Smith, Charley 16, 113
Smith, Jackie *123*, 123-24
Smith, Riley *35*, 36
Smith, Red 81
Snell, Matt 110, *111*, 112
'Snow Bowl' 135-36, *136*
Southern California Trojans Wisconsin **1963** Rose Bowl *91*, 91-2, *92*
Southern Methodist University Mustangs *63*, 63
Speedie, Mac 57, 58, 59, 60
Spinney, Art 78
Stabler, Kenny 113
Stallworth, John 121, *122*, 122
Stanford University 18, *19*, 44, 90
Starr, Bart 10, 81-2, *82*, 83, 84, *86*, 86, 88, *89*, 89, *99*, 94, 95, *96*, 98, 101, 102-07, *104*, *107*
Staubach, Roger *121*, 121, 123, 124
Stebbins, Harold *42*, 42
Steffy, Joe *54*
Stephenson, Gil 67
Stout, Elmer 69
Stram, Hank 98, 99
Strock, Don 127-28, *128*, 133
Strong, Ken *28*, 29, *30*
Stuart, Bobby 54
Stuhldreher, Harry *19*, 19
Sugar Bowl 1936 *34*
Summerall, Pat 76, 77
Super Bowl game 10, 94, *97*, 97, *99*, *101*, 108, 116; origin 94; I *97*, 97-101; III 110-12, *111*, *112*; VII *3*, *116*, 117-20, *117*, *118*, *120*; XIII *4*, 121-24, *121*, *122*, *123*, *124*
Sutherland, Jock 40, *41*, 42
Swann, Lynn 121, *124*, 124
Swiacki, Bill 52, 54, *55*

T formation 42, 44-7, 63
Taylor, Jim 83, 84, *86*, 86, 88, *89*, *95*, *96*, 99, 102
Taylor, Otis 97, 98
Texas Christian University 40
Texas, University of 18
Thorpe, Jim 14-17, *15*, *16*, *17*
Thurston, Fred 86, 99, 103
Tittle, Y A 72, *83*, 83, *84*, 84, 86
Toledo Maroons 17
Townes, Willie 103, 107
Triplett, Mel 76
Truman, Harry S 67, *68*
Tucker, Young Arnold *49*, *50*
Tunnell, Emlen 86
Turner, Bulldog *45*, 46
Turner, Jim 111, 112
Twilley, Howard 119-20

UCLA Bruins 91
Unitas, Johnny *72*, 72, *73*, 73, 76-9, *79*, 94, 102, 108, *112*, 112

Van Buren, Steve 58, *59*
Van Brocklin Norm *59*, 59
VanderKelen, Ron *92*, 92
Villanova University 52
Volonnino, Bob *69*
von Schamann, Uwe 132-33, *133*

Waldorf, Lynn 62
Walker, Doak 72
Wallace, Francis 48-9
Ward, Arch 56
Washington Huskies 41
Washington Redskins 34, 35-7, 59; Bears **1937** *35*, **1940** *44*, 44-7, *46*; Dolphins 117-20
Waterfield, Bob *58*, 59, 60
Webster, Alex 72, 76, 84
Western Conference 59, 72; title 83, 88, 94, 95, 102
Wilkin, Wee Willie *46*
Wilkinson, Bud 62
Williams, Bob *63*, 65
Williams, Sam 88
Williamson, Fred 97, 98, 101
Willis, Bill 57
Wilson, Ben 92
Wilson, George *45*, 45, 88
Wilson, Willie 92
Winslow, Kellen 128, 132, 133
Wisconsin Badgers, University of *70*; S Cal **1963** Rose Bowl 91-2, *92*
Wood, Willie 101, 104
Woodley, David 127, *128*
Workman, Vince *140*
Wright, Randy 121, 124

Yablonski, Ventan 54, 55
Yale University 8, *9*, 18
Yepremian, Garo 117, 120
Yost, Fielding 18, 20, *22*, 22

Zastrow, Bob 67, 68, *69*, 69
Zuppke, Bob 20, *22*, 22

Acknowledgments
The author and publisher would like to thank Design 23 who designed the book, Cynthia Klein who prepared the index, Jean Chiaramonte Martin and Donna Cornell Muntz who did the picture research and John Kirk, the editor.

Picture Credits

All-Sport (UK) Ltd.: page 7 (both).
The Bettmann Archive Inc.: pages 6, 8, 9 (top right and bottom), 10 (bottom), 14 (top), 17 (bottom), 18 (top), 24 (top), 90.
Bison Picture Library: page 10-11.
Chance Brockway: pages 134-35, 136 (top), 138, 139 (both), 140-41 (all three), 142.
Chicago Bears: pages 37, 44, 47 (top left).
Focus On Sports: pages 3, 4-5, 97 (both), 98, 99 (both), 100-01, 104 (top), 105, 108-09, 109 (top), 110-11 (all three), 112 (both), 113 (both), 114, 115 (bottom), 116 (both), 117, 118 (both), 119, 120 (both), 121 (both), 122, 123 (both), 124, 125, 126, 127 (both), 129 (both), 132 (both), 133 (both).
The Ohio State University Photo Archives: pages 136 (bottom), 137 (both).
Pro Football Hall of Fame: pages 14 (center), 15 (both), 24 (bottom), 26 (both), 30 (bottom), 36, 48 (top), 56 (both), 57 (left), 59 (right), 73 (top), 80 (both), 82, 83 (both), 84, 87 (both), 94 (top).
Purdue University Athletic Public Relations: page 64.
Stanford Sports Information, Stanford University: pages 19 (right), 45 (top).
University of Illinois: page 22 (top).
UPI/Bettmann Newsphotos: pages 1, 9 (top left), 12, 13 (both), 16, 17 (top), 18 (bottom), 19 (left and center), 20-21 (both), 22 (bottom), 23, 35 (both), 27, 28, 29, 30 (top), 31 (both), 32, 33 (both), 34, 35 (both), 38-39, 40, 41 (both), 42-43 (all three), 45 (bottom), 46 (top), 46-47, 47 (top right), 48 (bottom), 49 (both), 50 (both), 51, 52, 53 (both), 54-55 (all three), 57 (right), 58 (left), 58-59, 60, 61, 62, 63 (both), 65, 66 (both), 67, 68 (both), 69 (all four), 70 (both), 71, 72 (left), 72-73, 73 (bottom right), 74-75, 76, 77, 78-79 (all three), 81, 84 (bottom left and right), 84-85, 85 (bottom left and right), 86 (both), 88-89 (all three), 91 (both), 92, 93, 94 (bottom left), 94-95, 95 (top), 96, 102-03, 104 (bottom), 106-07, 107, 109 (bottom right), 115 (top), 128, 130-31.